FALSE CONSCIOUSNESS

FALSE CONSCIOUSNESS

An Essay on Mystification

Guenter Lewy

Transaction Books
New Brunswick (U.S.A.) and London (U.K.)

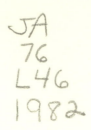
Library of Congress Catalog Number: 82–1985
ISBN: 0–87855–451–3
Printed in the United States of America

Library of Congress Cataloging in Publication Data
Lewy, Guenter, 1923–
   False consciousness.

   Includes bibliographical references and index.
   1. Political socialization   2. Consciousness.
3. Political socialization — Communist countries.
4. Capitalism. 5. Democracy. I. Title.
JA76.L46   303.3′7   82–1985
ISBN 0–87855–451–3   AACR2

Table of Contents

Preface

The idea of writing this book developed during the late 1960s and early 1970s when a large number of graduate students I taught became taken by the Marxian notion of "false consciousness" — the idea that people under capitalism lead a manipulated existence and do not know their own best interests. Influenced by Herbert Marcuse and other theorists of the New Left, these students often used the concept of false consciousness as a glib and convenient label for popular opinion that did not follow leftist prescriptions. Despite the popularity of the idea of false consciousness, most of these young people knew little about its origin or about its use in communist countries or about socialization in Western societies, which they condemned for fostering mystification. I therefore decided that an examination of these issues might be useful.

Today one hears less about false consciousness, though the question whether, or to what extent, people can be regarded as the best judges of their own interests remains, of course, a central concern of political philosophy. On the other hand, the events of 1980–81 in Poland have once again reminded the world that the Marxian dictum "Being Determines Consciousness" does not hold even in the so-called socialist countries where Marxism is the reigning ideology. As earlier in Hungary and Czechoslovakia, the Polish workers, too, did not regard the communist state as the guardian of their true interests and they organized massive strikes against it. Strikes, according to communist teachings, are a consequence of the class struggle under capitalism. When they occurred in a supposedly socialist society they were dismissed by Russian propaganda as a result of agitation by the enemies of socialism and as a reappearance of false consciousness. Once again, then, this venerable concept had to serve as an alibi for the failure of Marxian theory and practice.

This is a short book that deals with a subject of numerous and very wide ramifications. Each of the eight chapters of this book could easily have been expanded into a full-scale study in its own right. In the interest of a compact presentation and in order to focus on the central issue of interest to me, I have severely limited my discussion of matters only indirectly related to the main subject; because of this limitation of scope I have called this book an essay. I am interested here neither in providing a definitive history of the idea of false consciousness nor in analyzing in detail all the many complex philosophical issues raised by this concept. For example, throughout the essay I have accepted, without offering full supporting arguments, the meta-ethical position of noncognitivism; i.e., that moral principles do not have cognitive status, cannot be said to be either true or false, and that there therefore is no such thing as "moral truth." My main aim has been to apply what German scholars call *Ideologiekritik* to the Marxian concept of ideology or false consciousness itself, to demystify the concept of mystification.

The argument of this essay proceeds as follows: In chapter 1 I present an account of the historical development of the concept of false consciousness. The next three chapters (Part II) depict attempts to eliminate false consciousness in the Soviet Union, the People's Republic of China, and by Marxists and other radicals in the educational system of the Federal Republic of Germany. Since "emancipatory pedagogy" is relatively little known outside of Germany, chapter 4 is longer and more detailed than the other two chapters of this section that describe more familiar practices. Part III deals with the charge that the American people are manipulated by dominant groups into supporting the political, social, and economic principles governing this society and thus suffer from false consciousness. In order to evaluate this allegation I examine the role of education and the mass media in influencing basic political attitudes and social values. This examination, utilizing some of the most recent social scientific evidence available, yields the conclusion that the American system of education and the media of communication do not create or strengthen the cultural hegemony of a ruling class. Educational institutions, the press, radio, and television, it turns out, do not program people to embrace capitalist democracy and do not force upon them a false consciousness. On the contrary, it appears that both educational institutions and the media often are in the forefront of challenging the status quo and contribute to social change and the weakening of traditional values. The existence of such pluralism in itself does not refute the charge of false consciousness, but it calls into question the allegation of a one-dimensional manipulation of public opinion. In the body of the book (chapters 1–7) I combine the exposition of ideas and the description of political realities with a brief critique of some theoretical premises. In the concluding section, chapter 8, I undertake a more thorough theoretical analysis of the concept of false consciousness and of its implications for our contemporary democratic society.

Chapter 4 of this book was published in a slightly different form as an article, "The Persisting Heritage of the 1960s in West German Higher Education," in *Minerva* (London), vol. XVIII, no. 1 (Spring 1980), and is reprinted here with permission of the editor of *Minerva*. Field research in Germany for this chapter was made possible by a grant from the Earhart Foundation for which I express my gratitude.

I also want to thank my colleagues and friends Brigitte and Peter L. Berger, William E. Connolly, Paul Hollander, Christopher J. Hurn, and Stanley Rothman for their critical reading of the manuscript. The responsibility for whatever shortcomings remain is mine.

Northampton, Mass.
September 1, 1981

PART I

The Theory of False Consciousness

CHAPTER 1

False Consciousness: From Marx to Marcuse

Antecedents of a notion of false consciousness can be found as far back as Plato's myth of the cave in Book VII of the *Republic*. Francis Bacon relied upon Plato's notion of false appearances when he developed his doctrine of "idols," errors into which the human mind is prone to fall and which impede human progress and scientific knowledge. However, it is the Marxian idea that the masses under capitalism suffer from false consciousness by not knowing their own best interests, which has had a lasting impact on modern revolutionary thought.

The Founders: Marx and Engels

The term "false consciousness" appears for the first time in a letter by Friedrich Engels to Franz Mehring written on July 14, 1893. "Ideology," Engels wrote, "is a process accomplished by the so-called thinker consciously, it is true, but with false consciousness. The real motive forces impelling him remain unknown to him: otherwise it simply would not be an ideological process. Hence he imagines false or seeming motive forces."[1] Ideological thinking is thinking that is ignorant of the true factors determining history. Ideologies look at the world as shaped by ideas whereas man's thinking is merely an echo of material conditions. In turn, such false consciousness leads to a failure to understand the direction in which history is moving and to ignorance of the correct role that the various classes have to play in the unfolding historical process.

Without using the term "ideology" or "false consciousness," Marx and Engels from their earliest writings on stressed the idea that men suffer from illusions and mystification that must be cleared away by philosophy. For example, in *The German Ideology*, written for the most part between September 1845 and the summer of 1846, they declared: "Hitherto men have constantly made up for themselves false conceptions about themselves, about what they are and what they ought to be. . . . Let us liberate them from the chimeras, the ideas, the dogmas, imaginary beings under the yoke of which they are pining away."[2] Two years earlier, in September

3

1843, in a letter to Arnold Ruge, Marx had set forth the same task: "The reform of consciousness consists *only* in making the world aware of its own consciousness, in awakening it out of its dream about itself, in *explaining* to it its own actions."[3]

False or illusory consciousness, in the Marxian view, afflicts all classes, though in different ways. For the bourgeoisie, as for all ruling classes, false consciousness hides the true nature of bourgeois class rule — from itself and from those whom it dominates and oppresses. Each new ruling class, Marx and Engels wrote in *The German Ideology*, "is compelled, merely in order to carry through its aim, to represent its interests as the common interest of all the members of society, that is, expressed in ideal form: it has to give its ideas the form of universality, and represent them as the only rational, universally valid ones."[4] Bourgeois false consciousness is a "selfish misconception" that considers the transitory capitalist mode of production and form of property the result of "eternal laws of nature and of reason."[5] Bourgeois false consciousness thus sustains the belief in the eternal rule of the bourgeoisie. It can do so because "the ideas of the ruling class are in every epoch the ruling ideas, i.e. the class which is the ruling *material* force of society, is at the same time its ruling *intellectual* force. The class which has the means of material production at its disposal, has control at the same time over the means of mental production." The individuals composing the ruling class "rule also as thinkers, as producers of ideas." Some of them function as "ideologists, who make the perfecting of the illusion of the class about itself their chief source of livelihood."[6]

False consciousness for the proletariat, on the other hand, involves the failure to recognize that the interests of the working class require the abolition of capitalism and that this revolutionary change will liberate not only the proletariat but society as a whole. "False consciousness, in this sense," Ralph Miliband correctly notes, "is also the failure to realize the universal task which the proletariat is called upon to perform. . . . The worker is falsely conscious when he fails to realize the universal nature of his role, the bourgeois because he fails to realize the partiality of his class."[7]

The proletariat, according to Marx and Engels, suffers from false consciousness at an early stage of its development as a class. The economic revolution wrought by capitalism at first transforms peasants into workers. "The combination of capital has created for this mass a common situation, common interests. This mass is thus already a class as against capital, but not yet for itself."[8] One of the forms in which this intellectual backwardness expresses itself is religion — "an inverted world consciousness." Religion, as Marx put it in a famous phrase, is "the opium of the people," which, by stressing the importance of salvation in the next world, provides man with an "illusory happiness" on earth.[9]

Only gradually, and after prolonged suffering and struggle, does the proletariat become a class conscious of its own class interests and of its unique role in history. This transformation of the proletariat into a revolutionary class, aware of its historical mission, is one of the inevitable results of the social changes brought about by capitalism. "The question is not," Marx and Engels emphasized, "what this or that proletarian, or even the whole of the proletariat at the moment *considers* as its aim. The question is *what the proletariat is,* and what, consequent on that *being,* it will be compelled to do."[10] Moreover, as the contradictions of capitalism become more pronounced, some sections of the ruling class, who have comprehended the direction of the historical process, make common cause with the proletariat and provide it with additional enlightenment. They join the socialists and communists, the theoreticians of the proletarian class. As history moves forward, these theoreticians "no longer have to seek science in their minds; they have only to take note of what is happening before their eyes and to become its mouthpiece."[11] Scientific socialism, as the theoretical expression of the proletarian movement, thus imparts to the proletarian class "a full knowledge of the conditions and of the meaning of the momentous act it is called upon to accomplish."[12] The theoretical conclusions of the communists, declared the *Communist Manifesto,* "are in no way based on ideas or principles that have been invented or discovered, by this or that would-be universal reformer. They merely express, in general terms, actual relations springing from an existing class struggle, from a historical movement going on under our very eyes."[13]

The Marxian theory of ideology or false consciousness is far less systematic than our brief summary here suggests. There are many ambiguities, problems of consistency, and logical difficulties to some of which we will return in our concluding chapter.[14] Among the more important questions that can be raised are the following:

1. Marx and Engels predicted that the proletariat in due course would acquire true revolutionary consciousness, but they did not make it clear when this act of maturing would occur. In an early work of 1845, *The Holy Family*, they asserted that "a large part of the English and French proletariat is already *conscious* of its historic task and is constantly working to develop that consciousness into complete clarity."[15] On the other hand, in *The German Ideology*, written about the same time, they argued that only in the course of the revolution will the proletariat rid itself "of everything that still clings to it from its previous position in society" and will adopt "communist consciousness."[16] Marx and Engels sometimes assumed that revolutionary consciousness would develop inevitably and on its own, while at other times they stressed the importance of revolutionary strategy.[17]

2. If all men see society through the distorting spectacles of self-interest, if all human thinking is ideological and represents false consciousness, why is the proletariat exempt from this rule governing human behavior? Marx and Engels

asserted that the proletariat is the first class in history to acquire an undistorted knowledge of social reality, but their argument that the proletariat, because of its special position in the social structure of capitalism, will free itself of ideological thinking and enjoy what Leszek Kolakowski has called a special "cognitive privilege," remains unsubstantiated and unconvincing.

3. Most basically, when Marx and Engels speak of false consciousness they do not mean by this an error in the cognitive sense. False consciousness for them is thinking that does not conform to their theory of history and their vision of the future of mankind, both of which contain strong moral overtones. But why should these underlying moral assumptions be considered true and those of their critics false? The Marxist distinction between false and true consciousness assumes a standard of moral truth the existence of which is nowhere demonstrated. As Raymond Aron has argued cogently:

> The *petit bourgeois* who refuses to be a proletarian, because he regards culture and sentiments as more important than the amount of his wages, may be cowardly or blind in the view of Marxists, but from the standpoint of logic he merely has a different scale of values. The proletarian who transforms his situation by religious faith, and looks forward to a future life, may be resigned and stupid in the eyes of the unbeliever, but the criticism is just as metaphysical as the belief. Logically, it is a matter of different conceptions of the world. All self-awareness, and consciousness of one's own situation, implies a metaphysic and a moral theory, and what Marx regarded as authentic reality is only the expression of a particular philosophy.[18]

Leninism

According to Marx and Engels, the proletariat eventually would acquire class consciousness and embrace the revolutionary cause; i.e., it would rid itself of false consciousness. This expectation, that the working class would increasingly commit itself to the revolutionary abolition of capitalism, was to be disappointed. During the last decades of the nineteenth century, many working-class parties in Europe took note of the rising standards of living of the proletariat and instead of clamoring for the destruction of the capitalist system they began to work for its improvement and reform. Representatives of the workers entered parliaments and some of them even became members of coalition governments. The goal of Marxian socialism began to recede; the achievement of social legislation became more important than agitation for revolution. This was the context in which Lenin undertook his revision of Marxist doctrine.

The loss of revolutionary ardor on the part of the European working-class movement had been welcomed by Eduard Bernstein and other so-called revisionists. Lenin's essay, "What is to be done?," written in 1902, was designed to refute a Russian revisionist group known as the "Economists." Lenin's attack on reformist ideas drew strength from the special conditions of illegality and oppression under which Russian Social Democracy was operating and which seemingly proved the futility of peaceful reform.

According to Lenin, the working class, "by its own effort, is able to develop only trade union consciousness, i.e. the conviction that it is necessary to combine in unions, fight the employers and strive to compel the government to pass necessary labour legislation, etc." Such a spontaneous working-class movement, trade unionism, meant the ideological enslavement of the workers by the bourgeoisie because it diverted them from the fight for the abolition of the capitalist system. Hence the task of the Social Democrats was to combat this spontaneity, to "take up the political education of the working class and the development of its political consciousness."[19]

Marx and Engels, too, had stressed the importance of socialist education and the role of intellectuals in developing the revolutionary consciousness of the workers. Lenin built on this foundation and greatly extended the importance of "the conscious element," the role of the Social Democrats who brought socialist consciousness to the proletariat. "Class political consciousness," he insisted, "can be brought to the workers *only from without*." Hence the crucial importance of leadership and of theory. "Without a revolutionary theory there can be no revolutionary movement." In turn, the development of this revolutionary theory was the province of a vanguard party, a party of professional revolutionaries.[20]

Lenin called socialist theory socialist ideology. The term ideology now no longer was synonymous with false consciousness and in Lenin's vocabulary assumed a neutral meaning. Bourgeois ideology, not ideology as such, was false. Indeed, socialist ideology was all-important: "To belittle the socialist ideology *in any way*, to *turn away from it in the slightest degree* means to strengthen bourgeois ideology."[21] In practice this emphasis on the crucial role of revolutionary theory meant the sharp distinction between the working class and the vanguard party, because only the latter had a correct understanding of socialist theory. It would be futile and stupid, Lenin argued in his polemic against the Mensheviks who opposed his concept of a centralized vanguard party, "to think that at any time under capitalism the entire class, or almost the entire class, would be able to rise to the level of consciousness and activity of its vanguard, of its Social-Democratic Party."[22]

This elitist element became a permanent and essential feature of Leninist theory and practice. Marxist theory defined the true interests of the working class and this theory could be fully grasped only by its vanguard, the communist party. It was this party, itself run strictly from the top down, which represented true revolutionary class consciousness, which would save the workers from the corrupting influence of false consciousness and thus would enable the proletariat to fulfill its great historical mission. At times, this meant standing up even "against the opinion of the majority of the workers and to defend the [real] historical interests of the proletariat, in spite of everything."[23] Knowledge of the "historical interests of the proletariat," as of Rousseau's general will, did not depend on the counting of votes. Indeed, sometimes even fellow Bolsheviks exhibited an incorrect comprehension of the line of march and had to be disciplined. The theoretical rationale for an all-wise leader, who periodically would purge the party of critics and independent elements, was thus established; it represents an important element of continuity between Lenin's ideas and Stalin's repressive practices. The process of substitutism, against which Trotzky had warned, followed its logical course: The correct revolutionary consciousness, according to Lenin known by a self-selected vanguard party, eventually became the exclusive possession of its inspired general secretary.

It is an ironic fact that a man who "out-Lenined" Lenin in the ruthless logic with which he defended the leadership role of the vanguard party himself eventually ran afoul of the Stalinist system of persecution. Georg Lukacs, who in 1923 had published his essays on *History and Class Consciousness*, 10 years later was made to repudiate this book as strengthening "the front of idealism [which] is the front of Fascist counterrevolution and its accomplices, the Social Fascists. Every concession to idealism, however insignificant, spells danger to the proletarian revolution."[24] Lukacs, who had helped justify the unrestricted dictatorship of the communist party, thus was forced by that same party into an abject act of self-degradation. It remains an open question whether the brutal frankness with which Lukacs had defended the dictatorial rule of the party over the masses has something to do with this repudiation.[25]

Class consciousness, Lukacs had argued in the early 1920s, was not identical with the thoughts of men on their condition in society. Proletarian class consciousness was not the same as the psychological consciousness of individual proletarians or even of the entire class. The subjective development of the proletariat lagged behind the objective crisis of society. Despite the highly precarious situation of capitalism, the proletariat was still caught in capitalist forms of thinking. The strength of reformist parties and trade unions was the direct result of the bourgeois mentality still holding sway over the proletariat.

The communist party alone, according to Lukacs, could overcome these limitations of individual consciousness, transcend the illusions of reification, and develop a correct and coherent theory of the world. The communist party was the first conscious step from the realm of necessity into the realm of freedom. Individual liberty was now subordinated to the collective will of the party — the mediating agent between man and history, individual proletarians, and the objective interests of the class. The forms of liberty existing in other organizations, whether bourgeois or opportunistic workers' parties, were mere "formal democracy" and false consciousness. The communist party, on the other hand, was the historical embodiment and active incarnation of class consciousness. At times, the party had to act contrary to the momentary desires of the masses. One could only hope that the masses would eventually come to recognize the correctness of the party's position — the objectification of their own will. "The Communist Party is an *autonomous form* of proletarian class consciousness serving the interests of the revolution."[26]

According to this view, the criterion of truth lies embodied in the party, whatever the zig-zag of its official party line. True liberty consists in the renunciation of individual, formal liberty and submission to the will of the party. As a recent critic has put it, the moral endorsement of the party is a sign of the worker's entry to a state of political grace. "To be fully class conscious *and* to dissent from the will of the party would amount to a contradiction in terms."[27] The individual members of the party are like children in need of a guiding hand. This guidance is provided by the party's infallible leadership; whoever dominates the party at any one point in time automatically also represents the true consciousness of the revolution. All others — outside of and inside the party — suffer from false consciousness.

Marx's idea of class consciousness now had indeed come a long way. "In the Marxian perspective," George Lichtheim has correctly noted, "the emancipation of the working class is the business of that class itself, and not of a revolutionary elite of intellectuals. The class no doubt has varying levels of consciousness, and socialists are called upon to work with the most advanced; but that is all. An elite which embodies a consciousness denied to the class is a concept that Marx would not have accepted."[28] Even after the death of Stalin, Lukacs never fully repudiated his own extreme Leninist views. In the preface of a new edition of his political works, published in 1967, Lukacs admitted again that *History and Class Consciousness* suffered from a "Hegelian distortion" by undervaluing the role of economics, but he insisted that not all of it was mistaken.[29] In a series of conversations with several German intellectuals, held in 1966, Lukacs accused capitalist advertising of manipulating the workers' consciousness and he restated his belief in the need to carry class consciousness into the working class.[30] The working class thus remains subordinated to the "rational consciousness" expounded by self-elected revolutionary intellectuals who have unravelled the meaning of history.

Karl Mannheim

In the sociology of knowledge of Karl Mannheim, as with Marx, all thinking is socially determined, though, unlike for Marx, the economic factor is no longer the most important or decisive in shaping man's ideas. The concepts of ideology and false consciousness, too, are retained. In certain situations, "the collective unconscious of certain groups obscures the real conditions of society both to itself and to others and thereby stabilizes it." An ideology is the outlook of ruling groups who "in their thinking become so intensively interest-bound to a situation that they are simply no longer able to see certain facts which would undermine their sense of domination." Another kind of thinking is called "utopian" and it, too, biases human understanding and thus represents false consciousness. Utopian thinking is that of "oppressed groups [who] are intellectually so strongly interested in the destruction and transformation of a given condition of society that they unwittingly see only those elements in the situation which tend to negate it. . . . In the utopian mentality, the collective unconscious, guided by wishful representation and the will to action, hides certain aspects of reality. It turns its back on everything which would shake its belief or paralyze its desire to change things."[31]

It is the task of the sociology of knowledge, Mannheim maintained, to unmask the hidden social determinants of human thinking and thus to seek to overcome them. Specifically, it is the mission of modern intellectuals, "a social stratum which is to a large degree unattached to any social class,"[32] to develop an understanding of society, to illuminate the nature of socially bound interests that shape and distort the thinking of all other social groups directly involved in the economic process.

We have here what some students of Mannheim have called the "Mannheim paradox." To measure the distortion of a given political interpretation, somebody must be in possession of objective knowledge, for, as one interpreter of Mannheim correctly points out, "a distorted view is a distortion of some reality and we cannot know the scope or direction of distortion unless we can consider it against a background of valid knowledge."[33] But if all human thinking is determined by the social location, how can intellectuals overcome this limitation? If all knowledge is limited by social conditioning, how can the sociologist of knowledge know this insight to be true? Robert Merton indeed suggests that Mannheim's attempt to anchor the validity of social thought in the classless position of socially unattached intellectuals represents an unsuccessful effort to rescue oneself from an extreme relativism and "parallel[s] Munchhausen's feat of extricating himself from a swamp by pulling on his whiskers."[34]

Defenders of Mannheim, on the other hand, argue that the sociology of knowledge, by pointing out the social connectedness of an idea, does not seek to imply its falsehood. "The sociology of knowledge prejudges neither the truth nor the falsity of an idea, much less does it undermine or debunk the possibility of making such a distinction."[35] Similarly, intellectuals are not an exalted class, privy to revelation. They merely have maximum opportunity, by virtue of their education and other factors, to transcend the limitations of their social moorings. Mannheim, it has been suggested, from the beginning was aware of the so-called Mannheim paradox and, successfully or not, tried to work his way through the problems raised by it.

There is general agreement that Mannheim's formulations are often imprecise, and this may account for the rival interpretations and judgments passed on his work. These disagreements can be left unresolved here, but worth noting is the attraction of Mannheim's thought for intellectuals. The sociology of knowledge, by emphasizing the social origin of ideas rather than their intrinsic value, plays a debunking role that is highly congenial to modern intellectuals, especially those on the Left. Put off by the crudities of Marx's economic determinism and disappointed by the bureaucratic rigidities of the Soviet Union, which no longer was seen as the promised land, many intellectuals in the 1960s began to regard themselves as a privileged group, free from the distorting spectacles of class interests. Intended for such a role by Mannheim or not, they began to consider themselves as having the special mission of liberating man in capitalist society from his myths and illusions.

The New Left

The New Left never represented a well-defined social movement with a distinct set of ideas. It attracted primarily university students and academics; opposition to the American war in Vietnam often was one of the few clear common ideological denominators. Another idea espoused by most theorists of the New Left was the notion of false consciousness that more than anything else seemed suited to devalue the democratic political system.

The political thought of Herbert Marcuse, probably the best-known theorist of the New Left, reveals the influence of Marx and Mannheim, as well as Freud. As a member of the Frankfurt Institute of Social Research in the 1930s, Marcuse participated in the critical examination of Marxism and positivism and he helped develop what later became known as the "Critical Theory" of the Frankfurt School. According to Marcuse, the goods and services provided by the capitalist welfare state "promote a false consciousness which is immune against its falsehood." The welfare state is a form of unfreedom, its pluralism is deceptive and ideological. "The fact that the vast majority of the population accepts, and is made to accept, this society does not render it less irrational and less reprehensible. The distinction between true and false consciousness, real and immediate interests, still is meaningful."[36] Contemporary industrial society is irrational and operates through the manipulation of human needs by vested interests. It encourages "false needs," such as consumption, in accordance with advertising and the compulsive desire for fun and relaxation. Rational individuals, once freed from indoctrination and manipulation by the mass media, will be able to recognize these needs as false and regressive and instead will opt for the fulfillment of true, progressive, and vital needs such as real peace and a minimum of toil and injustice.

For Marcuse neither the proletariat nor the communist party can provide a vehicle for change; both are integrated into the existing system and suffer from false consciousness. The universities alone can be relied upon to develop an emancipated and true consciousness, to remove the veil that hides the terrible features of an affluent yet repressive consumer society. A new radical Left is to assume the "task of *political education*, dispelling the false and mutilated consciousness of the people so that they themselves experience their condition, and its abolition, as vital need, and apprehend the ways and means of their liberation."[37] Words and images that feed false consciousness must be stopped through censorship, even precensorship. Groups of the Right that promote cruel and aggressive policies, armaments, and chauvinism should not benefit from toleration and freedom of speech and assembly. There was need also for "new and rigid restrictions on teachings and practices in educational institutions which, by their very methods and concepts, serve to enclose the mind within the established universe of discourse and behavior — thereby precluding a priori a rational evaluation of the alternatives." The distinction between true and false tolerance is to be made by those who have learned "to think rationally and autonomously," by "the democratic educational dictatorship of free men."[38]

The existing political system of the West Marcuse dismissed as a "pseudo-democracy," which stood in the way of radical change. In such a democracy with a totalitarian organization the opposition could not remain legal and lawful. There was need for direct action and uncivil disobedience in order to create a system of true and direct democracy. The present elites had to be replaced by an "intellectual elite," capable of "independent thought" and "rational analysis," even if the majority of the people failed to endorse it.[39] In addition to students, Marcuse hoped that the forces of the "Great Refusal" would include the people of Vietnam, Cuba, and China, the guerillas of Latin America, and the ghetto populations of the United States. These oppressed minorities, which struggled against false consciousness, had a natural right of resistance and could use violence to break the established chain of violence.

Critics of Marcuse have pointed to the pronounced elitism of his thought. "How has Marcuse acquired the right to say of others what their true needs are?" Alasdair MacIntyre has asked. "How has he escaped the indoctrination which affects others?"[40] Marcuse's catalogue of true and false needs is not self-evident and it is neither irrational nor self-contradictory to disagree with his picture of a humane society. Liberation from false consciousness was to be imposed by intellectuals who claimed to know moral truth; those who disagreed were dismissed as irrational and the victims of manipulation. Marcuse's indictment of contemporary industrial society, another critic pointed out, was rich on rhetoric but vague on facts and cases. "His authority on social affairs seems to be Vance Packard."[41] The allegation that modern industry has impoverished life is sheer romanticism. Today's mass culture, Edward Shils has argued, "is less damaging to the lower classes than the dismal and harsh existence of earlier centuries had ever been."[42]

From the communist camp has come a repudiation that is no less severe. Marcuse's theory, a German critic has maintained, is not truly Marxist. His "objective role" is that of being part of the cold war.[43] Marcuse's impact on the student movement, on the other hand, at first was strong. In the midst of the crisis over civil rights in the United States and the worldwide agitation against the American war in Vietnam, Marcuse's denunciations of pseudo-democracy and false consciousness fell on fertile soil. Marcuse's defense of the right of oppressed minorities to use extralegal means effectively counteracted the liberal tabu of resort to violence. When Andreas Baader, later a leading member of the terrorist Baader-Meinhof gang in West Germany, was tried in 1968 for setting fire to a department store, he invoked Marcuse's essay on "Repressive Tolerance."

Even before members of the radical student Left had moved from the use of violence against things to violence against persons, Marcuse had begun to criticize the mindless activism of some segments of the student Left. In the late 1970s Marcuse argued that terror was illegitimate as long as there existed legal possibilities of effective resistance.[44] But by that time, quite clearly, the sorcerer was no longer in control of his apprentices. The thesis of the mere formal or repressive character of democratic institutions had proven itself as a highly effective means of undermining and delegitimating liberal values. Very few disciples of Marcuse ultimately embraced terrorism, but practically all those who became urban guerillas had been influenced by Marcuse's teachings on Western pseudo-democracy.[45]

The Urban Guerillas of Germany and Italy

The decline of the radical student movement in Europe and the emergence from its ranks of urban terrorists provide the setting for the most recent, and probably final, chapter in the process of substitutism. Lenin and Lukacs had substituted the vanguard party for the working class as the bearer of true consciousness; Marcuse had put the revolutionary intellectual in the place of the communist party. The so-called Baader-Meinhof gang or Red Army Faction (RAF) in West Germany and the Red Brigades in Italy, for the most part composed of former students who have refused a return to normalcy, are convinced that their small bands of terrorists have become the vanguard of the struggle against false consciousness, capitalism, and the "formal democracy" that has coopted their erstwhile comrades.

The German Red Army Faction regards itself as the inheritor of the Leninist vanguard party with the historic role of acting on behalf of the proletariat until the latter has acquired true consciousness. "What for Lenin had been the Bolshevik cadre party is today, under the conditions of multinational organization of capital and the transnational structure of inward and outward imperialist repression, the organized proletarian counterforce emerging from the guerillas."[46] Even a few dozen determined fighters, it is claimed, can fundamentally change the political scene by getting the masses to back the necessity of armed struggle and thus set in motion their liberation.

The German urban guerillas reject the peaceful strategy of the communist party as inappropriate. In the major imperialist countries, they argue, the proletariat cannot become what Marx had called "a class for itself," i.e., a class possessed of revolutionary consciousness and prepared to abolish capitalism. In Germany today the consciousness of the people is "totally manipulated" and there is nothing on which the guerillas could build, not even democratic or republican traditions. "In the face of the perfection of imperialist rule, antiimperialist consciousness can develop only with great difficulty. Every day the masses are exposed to the *Bild-Zeitung* [a tabloid] . . . . The actions of the RAF aim at creating an antiimperialist consciousness."[47]

The RAF insists that their movement is neither Blanquist nor anarchist. They consider themselves Marxists and they hope that their armed struggle will prepare the way for a mass movement against the capitalist system. The purpose of this struggle is to attack the system of imperialism from behind, to assault the bases from which imperialism prepares its attacks against Third World national liberation movements. By attacking the state apparatus at specific points they hope to destroy the myth of its strength and invulnerability. Gradually, it is expected, the masses will be drawn into this struggle and a revolutionary consciousness based on "proletarian internationalism" will emerge. The armed struggle should be complemented by work in the factories, though the former is a precondition of the success of the latter. Eventually the small armed band will become a large people's army that will win the people's war.

The expectation of the RAF that their campaign of assassinations and bombings will radicalize the German masses has proven false, and the reaction of the Italian people to the campaign of violence waged by the Red Brigades has been similarly hostile. The Red Brigades, too, define themselves as a vanguard of the working class; the class struggle, they insist, must take the form of armed struggle.[48] "Extending combat activities, concentrating armed attack on the vital centers of the imperialist state, organizing the fighting communist party in the proletariat — that is the right road for preparing the final victory of the proletariat, for definitively annihilating the imperialist monster and for building a Communist society."[49]

The working class of West Germany and Italy shows no sign of following its self-proclaimed liberators and stubbornly remains caught in "false consciousness." Indeed, in none of the developed capitalist countries have the successive champions of true revolutionary consciousness — vanguard party, revolutionary intellectuals, or urban guerillas — succeeded in gaining the kind of mass following that would enable them to gain power. Several different ways of striving for emancipation from false consciousness will be the subject of our discussion in the following three chapters.

Notes

1. Karl Marx and Frederick Engels, *Selected Works*, vol. II (Moscow, 1951), p. 451.
2. Karl Marx and Frederick Engels, *The German Ideology: Part One* (New York, 1970), p. 37.
3. *Deutsch-Französische Jahrbücher* in Karl Marx and Frederick Engels, *Collected Works*, vol. III (New York, 1975), p. 144.
4. *German Ideology*, pp. 65–66.
5. *Manifesto of the Communist Party* in *Selected Works*, vol. I (Moscow, 1951), p. 47.
6. *German Ideology*, pp. 64–65.
7. Ralph Miliband, "Barnhave: A Case of Bourgeois Consciousness," in Istvan Meszaros, ed., *Aspects of History and Class Consciousness* (London, 1971), p. 23.
8. Karl Marx, *The Poverty of Philosophy* (Moscow, n.d.), p. 195.
9. Karl Marx, "Contribution to the Critique of Hegel's Philosophy of Right," in Karl Marx, *Early Writings*, trans. and ed. T. B. Bottomore (New York, 1964), pp. 43–44.
10. Karl Marx and Frederick Engels, *The Holy Family or Critique of Critical Critique* (Moscow, 1956), p. 53.
11. *Poverty of Philosophy*, p. 140.
12. Frederick Engels, *Socialism: Utopian and Scientific* in Marx and Engels, *Selected Works*, vol. II, 142.
13. *Selected Works*, I, 44.
14. Arne Naess in his *Democracy, Ideology and Objectivity* (Oslo, 1956) points out that Marx and Engels in *The German Ideology* use the term "Ideologie" about 50 times without giving a clear definition (p. 154). For a careful discussion of this and other loose ends, see Martin Seliger, *The Marxist Conception of Ideology: A Critical Essay* (London, 1977), chaps. 2–4.
15. *Holy Family*, p. 53.
16. *German Ideology*, pp. 93–94.
17. Cf. Alfred G. Meyer, *Marxism: The Unity of Theory and Practice* (Ann Arbor, Mich., 1963), pp. 97–98, 109.

18. Raymond Aron, *German Sociology*, trans. Mary and Thomas Bottomore (London, 1957), p. 64.
19. V. I. Lenin, *What Is To Be Done? Burning Questions of Our Movement*, in *Selected Works*, vol. I, Part 1 (Moscow, 1950), pp. 233–34, 244, 263.
20. Ibid., pp. 287, 227, 336.
21. Ibid., p. 244.
22. *One Step Forward, Two Steps Back: The Crisis in Our Party*, ibid., p. 471.
23. From a resolution about the role of communist parties in the proletarian revolution adopted by the Second Comintern Congress, Petrograd 1921, quoted by Alfred G. Meyer, *Leninism* (Cambridge, Mass., 1957), p. 33.
24. G. Lukacs in *Pod Znamenem Marksizma*, vol. IV (July–August 1934), p. 143, cited by Morris Watnick, "Relativism and Class Consciousness: Georg Lukács," in Leopold Labedz, ed., *Revisionism: Essays on the History of Marxist Ideas* (London, 1962), p. 148.
25. Neil McInnes, *The Western Marxists* (London, 1972), p. 119.
26. Georg Lukács, *History and Class Consciousness: Studies in Marxist Dialectics*, trans. Rodney Livingstone (Cambridge, Mass., 1971), pp. 318, 330.
27. Frank Parkin, *Marxism and Class Theory: A Bourgeois View* (New York, 1979), p. 154.
28. George Lichtheim, *Lukács* (London, 1970), p. 51.
29. Peter Ludz, ed., *Georg Lukács: Schriften zur Ideologie und Politik* (Neuwied and Berlin, 1967), preface; see also George H. R. Parkinson, ed., *Georg Lukács: The Man, His Work and His Ideas* (London, 1970), p. 15.
30. *Gespräche mit Georg Lukács* (Reinbek bei Hamburg, 1967), pp. 43, 69.
31. Karl Mannheim, *Ideology and Utopia: An Introduction to the Sociology of Knowledge*, trans. Louis Wirth and Edward Shils (New York, 1936), p. 40.
32. Ibid., p. 156.
33. William E. Connolly, *Political Science and Ideology* (New York, 1967), p. 77.
34. Robert K. Merton, *Social Theory and Social Structure*, rev. ed. (New York, 1957), p. 507.
35. A. P. Simonds, *Karl Mannheim's Sociology of Knowledge* (Oxford, 1978), p. 31.
36. Herbert Marcuse, *One-Dimensional Man: Studies in the Ideology of Advanced Industrial Society* (Boston, 1966), pp. 12, xiii.
37. *Counterrevolution and Revolt* (Boston, 1972), p. 28.
38. *A Critique of Pure Tolerance* (Boston, 1965), pp. 101, 106.
39. *An Essay on Liberation* (Boston, 1969), pp. 69–71.
40. Alasdair MacIntyre, *Herbert Marcuse: An Exposition and a Polemic* (New York, 1970), p. 72.
41. McInnes, op. cit., p. 156.
42. Edward Shils, *The Intellectuals and the Powers and Other Essays* (Chicago, 1972), p. 262.
43. Robert Steigerwald, "Ein Apostel des 'dritten' Weges: Zur Kritik der Theorie Herbert Marcuses," *Probleme des Friedens und des Sozialismus* (Prague), XII (1969): 1098.
44. Herbert Marcuse et al., *Gespräche mit Herbert Marcuse* (Frankfurt, 1978), p. 150.
45. Cf. Hermann Lübbe, *Endstation Terror: Rückblick auf Lange Märsche* (Stuttgart, 1978), p. 8.
46. Interview of inmate of Stammheim prison with *Der Spiegel*, January 20, 1975, *Texte der RAF* (Lund, 1977), pp. 253–54.

47. Ibid., p. 445.
48. Cf. Alessandro Silj, *Never Again Without a Rifle: The Origins of Italian Terrorism*, trans. Salvator Attanasio (New York, 1979), p. 205.
49. Statement of the Red Brigades, May 5, 1978, reprinted in the *New York Times,* May 6, 1978.

PART II

The Practice of Eradicating False Consciousness

CHAPTER 2

The Political Use of Psychiatry in the Soviet Union

Abuses of involuntary commitment to psychiatric institutions occur everywhere; the case of Ezra Pound is the best known American case in which the action of psychiatrists is suspected of having been influenced by political considerations. The Czarist police, too, labeled oppositionists as insane. For example, the philosopher Petr Yakolevich Chaadaev (1794–1856), who had denounced the tyranny of Nicholas I, was declared mad on orders of the Czar in 1836 and put under psychiatric house arrest for one year.[1] Yet in no other country has this practice become as common and systematic as in the Soviet Union. Dissidents from the prevailing political orthodoxy are said to be suffering from delusions of reformism, a form of schizophrenia requiring compulsory treatment in a psychiatric institution.

Theoretical Foundations

The "scientific" foundation for the commitment of political dissidents developed by Russian psychiatrists, on the most basic level, involves the Marxist concepts of economic determinism and class struggle. Thus, Professor Daniil Lunts, in his monograph *The Theory and Practice of Forensic-Psychiatric Diagnosis*, attributed crime to the social disharmony characteristic of capitalism. In a socialist society the social causes of criminal acts were said to have been eliminated and any illegal act therefore merits psychiatric analysis.[2] More specifically, Soviet psychiatrists make use of the Marxist theory of the link between being and consciousness. "Life is not determined by consciousness," Marx and Engels had written in *The German Ideology*, "but consciousness by life."[3] The same point was made by Marx some years later in the preface to *A Contribution to the Critique of Political Economy:* "It is not the consciousness of men that determines their being, but, on the contrary, their social being that determines their consciousness."[4] Hence, it is argued by Soviet theorists, in a socialist society there should be no such thing as nonsocialist consciousness; the human mind is a mirror of a nation's economic system. Under so-

21

cialism, manifestations of political dissidence are a surviving legacy of the capitalist past or a result of bribery by imperialist enemies or the product of mental illness. An antisocialist consciousness is therefore ipso facto false consciousness; those who persist in criticizing the socialist society in which they live must be cured of their mental aberration.

The policy of interning political dissenters in psychiatric institutions was begun in the late 1930s, though initially the intent was often benevolent — to spare the offender the ordeal of the forced labor camp.[5] During the last years of Stalin's life, various branches of science were subjected to political purges. In 1950, at a joint session of the Academy of Sciences and the Academy of Medical Science, a crude form of the doctrine of I. P. Pavlov (1849–1936) was elevated to the status of dogma; the consequent weeding out of "anti-Pavlovists" merged with the anti-Semitic campaign of 1951–52. Thereafter psychiatry was monopolized by the school of A. V. Snezhenevsky, who promoted a new unitary Pavlovian theory of schizophrenia. After Snezhenevsky had become head of the Department of Clinical Medicine of the Academy of Medical Science and chief psychiatrist of the Ministry of Health, his broad definition of schizophrenia, applied to a very wide range of behavior, became the prevailing orthodoxy.[6] During the period of relaxed political controls that followed the death of Stalin when the Soviet state did not want to stage too many trials of political opponents, Snezhenevsky's theory easily lent itself to use and abuse by the authorities. With its help, political dissidents could be found unfit to stand trial and instead committed to psychiatric institutions; this convenient way of eliminating dissenters has continued to be used to this day.

The center of the Snezhenevsky school is the V. P. Serbsky Institute of Forensic Psychiatry in Moscow whose current director is Dr. G. V. Morozov. Some of the key ideas of the Snezhenevsky school can be found in a book, *Nervous and Psychic Diseases*, coauthored by Morozov and V. A. Romasenko, the latter being chief of the Department of Pathological Morphology of the Institute of Psychiatry at the Soviet Academy of Sciences. According to the Snezhenevsky school, there exist three forms of schizophrenia: continuous, shift-like, and periodic. Subtypes of the continuous form are defined by the rate at which the disease progresses: rapid, moderate, and sluggish (or creeping). Dissenters are commonly classified as suffering from the sluggish or creeping form, the onset of which is "insidious" in that the patient retains full ability to function.[7] The great advantage of this typology is that it enables psychiatrists to label as insane individuals whose outward behavior is perfectly normal. Snezhenevsky and Morozov put it thus:

> There is a small number of mental cases whose disease, as a result of mental derangement, paranoia and other psychopathological symptoms, can lead

them to anti-social actions which fall in the category of those that are prohib-
ited by law, such as disturbance of public order, dissemination of slander,
manifestation of aggressive intentions, etc. . . . To the people around them
such mental cases do not create the impression of being obviously "insane."
Most often these are persons suffering from schizophrenia or a paranoid
pathological development of the personality. Such cases are known well both
by Soviet and foreign psychiatrists.

The seeming normality of such sick persons when they commit socially dangerous actions is used by anti-Soviet propaganda for slanderous contentions
that these persons are not suffering from a mental disorder.[8]

One of the symptoms of this type of schizophrenia is said to be the holding of "paranoid reformist delusional ideas" in which the patient grossly
overvalues his own importance and exhibits grandiose ideas of reforming
Soviet society and the world. In the words of Professors Pechernikov and
Kosachev of the Serbsky Institute:

Most frequently, ideas about a "struggle for truth and justice" are formed by
personalities with a paranoid structure. Litigiously paranoid states come into
being as a result of psychologically traumatic circumstances affecting the
subject's interests and are stamped by feelings that the individual's legal
rights have been infringed.

A characteristic feature of overvalued ideas is the patient's conviction of his
own rectitude, an obsession with asserting his "trampled" rights, and the significance of these feelings for the patient's personality. They tend to exploit
judicial proceedings as a platform for making speeches and appeals.[9]

The term "delusions of reconstruction or reformation" has been clarified
by another doctor of the Serbsky Institute in this way:

They deal with social problems. The patient thinks it necessary to reform the
system of government control in this country. He thinks that he himself is
capable of undertaking leadership; that it is necessary to review theoretical
problems of social science and that he himself is capable of explaining the
theory and practice of Soviet industry and reconstruction. His ideas are so
essential [he believes] that he should leave the Soviet Union and disseminate
them in all the countries of the world.[10]

In other case reports one finds similar symptoms of alleged illness:

He expresses with enthusiasm and great feeling reformist ideas concerning
the teaching of the Marxist classics, revealing in the process a clear overesti-
mation of himself and an unshakable conviction of his own rightness.

. . . delusional reformist ideas and an absence of criticism toward his own
condition and the situation which has developed.

His political thinking is grossly contradictory. He minimizes his actions and
does not comprehend their criminal treacherous nature. . . . He considers

himself to be a political figure of world-wide significance who will be defended by the Commission on Human Rights of the United Nations.[11]

The fact that the dissenters hold critical views of Marxism-Leninism or of the political and economic system of the Soviet Union and are unwilling to repudiate these "false beliefs" is considered proof of sickness. Their "reformism" is labeled delusional because these persons hold onto their beliefs with tenacity and, even in the face of "incontrovertible evidence," cannot be dissuaded from their false beliefs. The assumption is that the Soviet system is perfect and in no need of improvement; anyone insisting on its reform therefore suffers from delusions of reformism and is insane. False consciousness under the conditions of socialism is a mental disease.

Several Western psychiatrists, who have studied the Russian psychiatric literature and who have met the leading Soviet psychiatrists, doubt that the ruling theory of schizophrenia was developed with the aim of controlling political dissidents.[12] However, it is undisputed that the doctrines of the Moscow school of psychiatry, founded by Snezhenevsky, have been favored by the Communist party and the Soviet state and that those who accepted the broad view of schizophrenia propounded by that school have been selected for high positions. Altogether, the collaboration between psychiatrists and the political police probably is at least in part "a subtle, inexplicit process, wherein both parties share assumptions about what constitutes deviancy from conformist public behavior."[13] In a society where Marxism is the official ideology and where the boundaries of acceptable political conduct are far narrower than in the West, it is not surprising that many will readily come to believe that political dissenters are mentally ill. This explanation, as a Western psychiatrist, Dr. Walter Reich, has pointed out, is also easier on the ego:

> Seeing dissent as courage threatens one's own integrity. If to dissent is to be courageous, then in not dissenting one is a coward. But even more fundamentally, if the dissidents are right then the conventional views of conventional Soviet citizens are wrong. Acceptance of and reliance on the system are called into question. It is easier and more comforting to see the dissident as mentally ill, it is a relief to everyone — including the psychiatrists themselves, who are no less conventional than their lay comrades.[14]

The Psychiatric Gulag

The Serbsky Institute is nominally under the aegis of the Ministry of Public Health, but its so-called Special Section, which conducts the psychiatric examination of dissidents, includes representatives of the KGB. The late Professor Daniil Lunts, until his death in 1977 the head of the Special Section, is said to have been a psychiatrist as well as a KGB officer; several witnesses reported seeing him come to work in the uniform of a KGB colonel. Other members of this section, including nurses, are also thought to hold KGB rank. The "Special Psychiatric Hospitals," in which dissidents are confined, are similarly managed by the security forces of the Ministry of Internal Affairs (MVD), and their staffs are members of these security organs. The Serbsky Institute examines dissidents who live in Moscow or who have committed their offense there; it also functions as a final arbiter if a local forensic psychiatric commission has had the temerity to find an accused sane. Despite great pressure on psychiatrists in the provinces to toe the official line, such findings do occur occasionally.[15]

Until 1960, the criminal code made psychiatrists criminally liable for placing persons in psychiatric hospitals without adequate grounds. It also provided for recourse to the courts in contested cases. These provisions were omitted from the new criminal code of 1961. Another set of rules facilitating the compulsory commitment of political dissidents are the regulations governing "Emergency Hospitalization of Mentally Ill Persons Who are a Public Danger," issued by the Ministry of Health — after clearance with the Ministry of Internal Affairs, the Ministry of Justice, and the KGB — on October 10, 1961. After listing some of the grounds for commitment to a psychiatric institution, the regulations continue: "The morbid conditions enumerated above which can undoubtedly constitute a danger to the public, may be accompanied by externally correct behavior and dissimulation. . . . The grounds for compulsory hospitalization enumerated above are not exhaustive but only a list of the most frequently encountered morbid states which present a public danger."[16] In effect, these provisions enable psychiatrists to commit any person whom the authorities want to see committed. It becomes easy to assert that apparently normal citizens are in fact insane persons simulating normality. A special decree, issued jointly by the Minister of Public Health and the Minister of Internal Affairs on May 15, 1969, further broadened the category "socially dangerous behavior" by introducing the concept of "socially dangerous tendencies."[17]

With its emphasis on the biological basis of mental illness, Soviet psychiatry prefers tranquilizing and other drugs to psychotherapy. Some of these drugs cause extreme discomfort — headaches, fever, stomach cramps, convulsions, etc. — and are administered without corrective medications as a form of punishment for patients who refuse to cooperate with their doctors or fail to acknowledge their false beliefs. Prolonged treatment with some of these drugs has been known to lead to organic deterioration that is irreversible. Another type of punishment used is the "roll-up" in which the patient is tightly wrapped from feet to shoulder in a wet sheet or strips of canvas. As this material dries it shrinks and inflicts severe pain.[18] The acknowledgment of sickness and the repudiation of previous behavior are commonly demanded as a condition for discharge.

The total number of dissidents held in psychiatric institutions is not known with any precision. Several diagnostic projects, some of them organized by the World Health Organization, have shown that the diagnosis of schizophrenia is made in the Soviet Union far more often than in the rest of the world. More specific information comes from ex-patients who have left the Soviet Union, emigré psychiatrists who have corroborated the testimony of the patients, human rights organizations such as the Moscow Working Commission to Investigate the Use of Psychiatry for Political Purposes, Western journalists, and visiting Western psychiatrists. The young dissident Vladimir Bukovsky, who by 1971 had spent nine out of his 30 years of life in prisons and psychiatric hospitals, managed to send to the West a large number of psychiatric case histories. In 1975, Amnesty International published a study, *Prisoners of Conscience in the USSR*, which summarized much of the material available on the compulsory detention of political dissidents in psychiatric institutions. These reports, emanating from different sources and consistent in their particulars, by now have built a record that cannot easily be ignored.

One of the best known cases is that of former Major General P. G. Grigorenko, sentenced by the Serbsky Institute to an indefinite term in a special psychiatric hospital. Grigorenko was arrested in Tashkent, but since the evidence against him was found to be insufficient for a criminal trial he was put before a medical commission for a psychiatric examination. Unexpectedly the commission found him to be of sound mind and this finding was accepted by the Tashkent court. At this point, his case was transferred to the Serbsky Institute in Moscow where he was examined by a team of psychiatrists more experienced in political cases, including Doctors Morozov and Lunts. This new commission reviewed the findings of the Tashkent doctors and on November 11, 1969 found Grigorenko to be "not answerable for his actions" since he suffered from "a mental illness in the form of a pathological (paranoid) development of the personality, with the presence of reformist ideas. . . . Reformist ideas have taken on an obstinate character and determine the conduct of the patient."[19] After several years of confinement, Grigorenko eventually reached the West where he asked for and received a thorough psychiatric examination by a team of American psychiatrists. After lengthy interviews, neurological examinations, and batteries of psychological tests, the psychiatrists concluded that there was absolutely no evidence of mental illness.[20]

In all, the cases of about 300 victims of Soviet political psychiatry have been well documented.[21] Among well-known dissidents who have been subjected to compulsory psychiatric treatment are the geneticist Zhores A. Medvedev, mathematician Leonid Plush, linguist Tatyana Khodorovich, and writer Victor Nekipelov. As a result of pressure from the West, many of these dissidents were eventually released and allowed to emigrate. The chances of liberation for those less well known in the West are much slimmer. By July 1981, seven key figures of the Moscow Working Commission to Investigate the Uses of Psychiatry for Political Purposes had been sentenced to labor camps and exile ranging from three to 12 years. This stepped-up repression has effectively silenced the group's activities and has greatly complicated the West's efforts to keep informed of the abuses of psychiatry that continue to take place.[22]

Notes

1. Zhores A. and Roy A. Medvedev, *A Question of Madness,* trans. Ellen de Kadt (New York, 1971), pp. 136, 197. Several other cases are mentioned by Harvey Fireside, *Soviet Psychoprisons* (New York, 1979), pp. 12–13.
2. Cf. "A Manual on Psychiatry for Dissidents" compiled by Dr. Semyon F. Gluzman and Vladimir Bukovsky in 1974 and reproduced in Fireside, op. cit., pp. 92–118. Dr. Lunts' work is discussed on p. 99.
3. Karl Marx and Frederick Engels, *The German Ideology: Part One* (New York, 1970), p. 47.
4. Karl Marx, Preface to *A Contribution to the Critique of Political Economy,* Karl Marx and Frederick Engels, *Selected Works,* vol. I (Moscow, 1951), p. 329.
5. Sidney Bloch and Peter Reddaway, *Psychiatric Terror* (New York, 1977), pp. 51–53.
6. Medvedev and Medvedev, op. cit., pp. 68–69.
7. Victor Nekipelov, *Institute of Fools,* trans. Marco Carynnyk and Marta Horban (New York, 1980), p. xxii.
8. Letter to the *Guardian,* September 29, 1973, cited by Malcolm Lader, *Psychiatry on Trial* (Hammondsworth, 1977), pp. 137–38.
9. Cited by Vladimir Bukovsky, *To Build a Castle: My Life as a Dissenter,* trans. Michael Scammel (New York, 1979), p. 357.
10. John Kenneth Wing, *Reasoning About Madness* (Oxford, 1978), p. 189.
11. Cited by Bloch and Reddaway, op. cit., pp. 251–52.
12. Wing, op. cit., p. 189; Walter Reich, "Diagnosing Soviet Dissidents," *Harper's* (August 1978), p. 35.
13. Fireside, op. cit., p. 60.
14. Reich, op. cit., p. 36.
15. Lader, op. cit., p. 149.
16. Medvedev and Medvedev, op. cit., p. 148.
17. U.S. Senate, Committee on the Judiciary, Subcommittee to Investigate the Administration of the Internal Security Act and Other Internal Security Laws, *Abuse of Psychiatry for Political Repression in the Soviet Union,* Hearings, 92nd Cong., 2nd sess., September 26, 1972, pp. 24–25.
18. Bukovsky, op. cit., p. 206; Nekipelov, op. cit., pp. xxii-xxiii.
19. Lader, op. cit., p. 125. The full text of two psychiatric evaluations by Soviet psychiatrists is reproduced in the Senate Judiciary Committee hearings cited in note 17 above.
20. Walter Reich, "Grigorenko Gets a Second Opinion," *New York Times Magazine,* May 13, 1979.

21. Peter Reddaway, "Psycho-Suppression," *New York Review of Books,* March 20, 1980.
22. John F. Burns, "Moscow Silencing Psychiatry Critics," *New York Times,* July 26, 1981.

CHAPTER 3

Thought Reform in the People's Republic of China

One of the contributions of Leninism to Marxist theory is the stress on the importance of revolutionary consciousness injected into the masses by the vanguard party in order to prepare them for their mission of overthrowing the capitalist system. This same emphasis on the volitional role in the making of the revolution reappears in Maoism and indeed is carried several steps further. According to Mao Zedong, not only the proletariat but all classes must be taught correct thinking; after the victory of the revolution, even people with improper class origins can and should be reeducated and imbued with socialist consciousness. This striving for ideological purity is one of the foundations for the Chinese practice of thought reform or thought struggle, the most ambitious attempt ever made to create not only a new society but also a new man.

Origins

Marxism-Leninism with its belief in the class character of ideological truth is one of the bases of the Chinese theory of thought reform; the borrowing from Russian communist theory and practice can be seen in the way thought reform is carried out. We find the same stress on criticism and self-criticism, a method of social control employed not only to ensure adherence to the party line but also to combat individualism and privacy and to subordinate all nonpolitical ties and relationships such as personal friendships to the interests and demands of the party.[1] The methods employed to extract confessions from recalcitrants resemble the techniques used by the Russians during the purge trials of the 1930s and by the East European communists in the purges undertaken after World War II. But whereas communist countries other than China have employed these methods of persuasion and pressure primarily within the ruling communist party, especially during recurring purges of oppositionists, the Chinese communists have undertaken the far more far-reaching program of reforming the thought of the whole society, to reeducate all members of the state.

29

While all totalitarian systems are obsessed with the passion for unanimity — manifesting itself in mass parades and demonstrations, and elections
with predetermined favorable results approaching 100 percent, etc.[2] — the
scope and intensity with which the Chinese communists have pursued the
goal of changing the mode of thinking of an entire people may have additional roots in Chinese culture. That tradition emphasizes a striving for
complete harmony as well as learning by rote and repetition. For example,
in his essay "How to be a Good Communist," Liu Shaoqi exhorted new
members of the party to pursue diligently their "self-cultivation," and he
held up as an example to be followed the life of Confucius: "At fifteen, I
had my mind bent on learning. At thirty, I stood firm. At forty, I had no
doubts. At fifty, I knew the decree of Heaven. At sixty, my ear was an obe-
dient organ for the reception of truth. At seventy, I could follow my heart's
desire, without transgressing what was right."[3]

Mao Zedong believed that wrong ideas were an illness that had to be
cured. In a speech given in 1942 before party members, Mao explained
that the "object in exposing errors and criticizing shortcomings is like that
of a doctor in curing a disease. The entire purpose is to save the person, not
to cure him to death. If a man has appendicitis, a doctor performs an oper-
ation and the man is saved. . . . We cannot adopt a brash attitude toward
diseases in thought and politics, but [must have] an attitude of 'saving men
by curing their diseases.' "[4] The ideological struggle carried out by the
party against bourgeois and other wrong ways of thinking was to inculcate
the correct socialist consciousness. "Once the correct ideas characteristic
of the advanced class are grasped by the masses, these ideas turn into a
material force which changes society and changes the world."[5]

"Thought Struggle"

Until the Communists seized power in China in 1949, the struggle
against wrong ideas such as idealism, individualism, absolute egalitarian-
ism, and ultra-democracy was waged within the ranks of the party in order
to forge unity and maintain the rigid discipline demanded by the principle
of democratic centralism. After 1949 this "thought struggle" was extended
to the entire population; the military victory was to be consolidated with
"victory on the ideological front." The liberated people were to be enabled
to "reform their bad habits and thought derived from the old society." A
nationwide study movement was launched to indoctrinate the population
with Marxism-Leninism; i.e., with correct thought. With minor changes in
form and focus, this ideological struggle against impure ideas has continued to this day; it constitutes the essence of the Chinese program of
thought reform.[6]

Almost from the beginning the ideological struggle paid special attention to the intellectuals — immersed in unproletarian ideas and caught up in the lies of the bourgeois class — who were expected to resist the indoctrination and propaganda effective with the uncritical masses. "Thought reform, especially the thought reform of the intellectuals," Mao declared in 1951, "is one of the most important prerequisites for the realization of democratic reform and industrialization."[7] Since the social system was now socialist, even intellectuals could adopt a socialist consciousness. They should be helped to shed their bourgeois world outlook and acquire the correct socialist view of the world. "Not to have a correct political point of view is like having no soul." This ideological remolding would take time and was to utilize persuasion, not compulsion. The struggle against bourgeois thinking was to be resolute but based on "painstaking reasoning and not crude coercion."[8] In practice, the techniques of reform, especially when employed against class enemies, often were far more coercive than this and other programmatic statements would indicate. As a result, in particular during the early years of the Communist regime and again later during the Cultural Revolution which began in 1965, many thousands are said to have been killed or tortured to death at mass rallies and in prisons.[9] During these years of upheaval, thought reform also led to numerous nervous breakdowns and suicides. Among the latter was Lao She, perhaps this century's outstanding Chinese humorist, who killed himself after being "struggled" by Red Guards in 1966.[10]

From the first great wave of reform on, which began in 1951 and emphasized the struggle against bourgeois ideas among the intellectuals, the process of thought reform has utilized the small group (*hsiao-tsu*) as the main vehicle of indoctrination. All adults belong to one or more small groups of about 10 to 20 members, based on their place of employment or residence, and these groups, led by a cadre, engage in a specified number of hours of "study" (*hsueh hsi*) each week. The technique of criticism and self-criticism utilized is borrowed from the Soviet Communist party, but unique is the extension of this practice to the whole society. Until the Cultural Revolution, it has been reported, in some instances there was a tendency for the thought reform process to become formalistic and to produce routinized responses. "Group members would soon learn what it was appropriate to say in particular circumstances. The study sessions tended to become just one more part of the regular work routine."[11] During the Cultural Revolution the *hsiao-tsu* network largely disintegrated in the general turmoil of the times, but since then it has been reestablished and indeed extended, sometimes down into individual families.[12] There is no indication that the death of Mao in 1976 and the consequent downfall of the "Gang of Four" have brought a change in this all-pervasive system of social control.

All education and socialization processes everywhere contain elements of coercive persuasion and indoctrination. But in Communist China the objects of education in the study groups are not children but adults whose mode of thinking is to be shaped into the mold desired by the ruling party. Thought reform involves not only developing loyalty and devotion to the country's leaders and insuring compliance with their directives, it also "entails changing a broad spectrum of attitudes, habits, inclinations, and desires in order to produce 'new men,' individuals willing to work hard, to struggle creatively to overcome obstacles, and to devote themselves to broad organizational and national goals without concern for individual advancement or comfort."[13] In view of the smallness of the group, escape from supervision and "help" is nearly impossible; the discovery of deviation from the standard of truth set by the party is certain. The visibility of thought is maximized by the fact that the groups contain overlapping memberships. Group leaders have access to superior authorities who supervise more than one group; the notes collected and passed up the supervisory chain from the multiple groups to which an individual belongs are likely to reveal any inconsistencies of thought and lead to corrective action.[14]

Detailed reports on the work of these groups have come to the West from refugees and foreigners with many years of life in Communist China.[15] A good description is provided by A. Doak Barnett:

> The pattern of discussion in the groups has peculiarities of its own. "Free discussion" and strict control are combined in a unique formula. Abstract theory is linked to personal attitudes and experience. Criticism and self-criticism are used to bring all members of the group into a complicated interrelationship in which they exert a mutual influence upon each other. The confessions involved in self-criticism give the discussion a strong emotional flavor, making it something quite different from a primarily intellectual discussion.
>
> One fundamental premise of all the discussions is that for every problem or question there is a "correct" solution or answer. The "truth" is contained in "scientific Marxism," as defined by the Party, and the problem is to understand and accept the Communists' basic theories of historical and social change, to relate these to current social, economic, political, and international issues, and to adapt one's own behavior to this theoretical framework. It is also assumed that no one — even old Party members — has progressed as far as is theoretically possible in understanding this "truth" and in fully relating one's personal life to it.
>
> This means that for average members of a *hsueh hsi* group, the whole aim of discussion is focused upon the necessity of repudiating past beliefs, discovering what it is that the Communist regime now requires them to believe, rejecting all competing ideas, and expressing — at least verbally — full acceptance of the "correct" dogma.[16]

Thought Reform for the Enemies of the Revolution

Those who refuse to think the correct thoughts, or class enemies who resist the revolution, when not executed, are imprisoned and put through a more intensive kind of thought reform. The majority of these offenders are subjected to forced labor, the purpose of which is described in the legislation as "to punish all counter-revolutionary and other criminal offenders and to compel them to reform themselves through labour and become new men."[17] During this time of "reform through labour," which is served in prison-factories, prison-farms, or so-called labour reform brigades, at least one hour a day is set aside for thought reform. Groups average 10 to 15 inmates and generally are led by prisoners with a good class or political background who have received relatively short sentences; some of these leaders are former cadres or party members. The texts "studied" are extracts from editorials or articles of political significance, and summaries of official reports on party congresses or national conferences. Notes taken during the study period are forwarded to an "instructor" who supervises the study groups and who may point out a lack of understanding or improper thoughts and request an acknowledgment of the mistakes made. The next session may then be used by the group leader for an admonishment of the backward prisoner who will be asked to make a thorough self-criticism. Prisoners who show insufficient remorse are vigorously critized by the other members of the group until they admit their wrong thoughts or they may be punished by a period of solitary confinement or by a reduction of food rations. Members of the group are also expected to denounce unorthodox thoughts or any other misdeed of their fellow prisoners that they may have observed.[18]

One study session a week is usually devoted to a general "self-examination" during which prisoners review their behavior during the preceding week. Here they must not only acknowledge their faults but also explain why they did wrong. A prisoner who fails to see any misdeeds in his conduct will be helped by the group leader or the other inmates. The notes taken during such meetings become part of the prisoner's file. Periodically, the behavior of the prisoners is also made the subject of a more general examination initiated by the director of the institution. During these evaluations, which can last several days or weeks, work may be reduced. Again, prisoners must engage in self-examination, mutual denunciation, confession of crimes, and admission of guilt. Inmates who reveal bad behavior or improper attitudes are subjected to "struggle" sessions.

The "struggle" is a practice developed by the Communists in the 1930s when they began to make headway in China's rural areas. It became the standard technique for interrogating landlords or other enemies who had fallen into their hands. The purpose was to make the class enemy confess, and this was achieved by bringing the man into an open area where he was forced to kneel and bow his head while dozens, hundreds, or thousands of peasants surrounded him. Screamed at, spat upon, slapped or beaten, and terrorized in this way, few victims could resist very long. Later the struggle came to be used in prisons and labor camps (and occasionally even in ordinary civilian life during special mobilization campaigns like the Cultural Revolution) as punishment for incorrect thoughts or in order to extract confessions. The following description of the institution of the struggle comes from a Chinese whose father was a French citizen, and who eventually was allowed to leave China after spending seven years in various labor camps:

> If a denunciation leads to a Struggle, the victim is well advised to submit immediately, because there is never any time limit to a Struggle: It can go on indefinitely if the leaders of the game feel that not enough contrition has developed. Like all the other non-physical interrogation techniques, the purpose is to bring the victim to accept anything that may be judged for him. Thus a Struggle is rarely resolved quickly; that would be too easy. At the beginning, even if the victim tells the truth or grovellingly admits to any accusation hurled at him, his every word will be greeted with insults and shrieks of contradiction. He is ringed by jeering, hating faces, screaming in his ear, spitting; fists swipe menacingly close to him and everything he says is branded a lie. At the end of the day he is led to a room, locked up, given some food and left with the promise that the next day will be even worse.
>
> Often there will be a day off, on Sundays for instance, but this, too, is an exercise in sadism. Locked in his room, he will be perpetually surveyed by at least one of the Struggle team. If he happens to look out the window, the guard will rebuke him for allowing his mind to wander from his problems, which must totally occupy his thoughts. If he nods off to sleep, the guard will grab him by the hair and jerk him awake. After three or four days the victim begins inventing sins he has never committed, hoping that an admission monstrous enough might win him a reprieve. After a week of Struggling he is prepared to go to any lengths.[19]

The struggle is also used during the period of interrogation that precedes trial and sentencing. Here it functions as one of several outright coercive techniques employed, which may include nonstop interrogation, verbal abuse, threats of violence, being forced to stand for long periods, deprivation of sleep, use of handcuffs and chains, and, occasionally, severe beatings. During this period of interrogation, which can take months and in special cases years, prisoners are fed a starvation diet — "enough to keep us alive but never enough to let us forget our hunger."[20] Daily study sessions sometimes take up most of the waking day; reports on these sessions become part of the prisoner's dossier. The overall purpose is to make the prisoner confess and show full repentance. True repentance is proven, among other ways, by pressuring others to confess and by showing the necessary enthusiasm at struggle sessions. Until all bad thoughts are bared, confessions must be written and rewritten. Eventually, the broken prisoner will thank his jailers for the sentence given him.

Some sentences are open-ended and prisoners are promised leniency if they make good progress in reforming themselves. On the other hand, bad behavior is met with an additional period of confinement. Some prisoners succeed in fooling their captors by confessing to crimes they never committed; they go through the motions of repeated full confessions without succumbing to the brainwashing to which they are exposed. A young woman, imprisoned for five years in labor camps on the charge of being part of a Catholic spy ring, reports that eventually she learned what was expected of her — she was released after writing a confession that benefited from the "higher level of political consciousness" she had acquired during the course of her confinement.[21] On the other hand, in some cases the conversion achieved is genuine and permanent. Two Americans, who spent four years in a Chinese prison, after their release and return to the United States published a book in which they sang the praise of the Chinese Revolution. One of them reported that he had changed his ideas "due to a perfectly rational process of examining my thoughts, testing them in the light of objective facts and moral principles, and arriving at new conclusions where I felt my former ones were wrong." Thought reform in China, they wrote, "has been instrumental in producing an entirely new Chinese society and a new Chinese man." What "we have learned during our prison experience has made us far happier and more active people than we otherwise would have been."[22] We do not know how many Chinese have been made similarly "happier and more active people" as a result of undergoing thought reform.

How Successful Has Thought Reform Been?

The total number of inmates of Chinese prisons and labor camps is not known and there exist no statistics on the number of locations or places of detention. Still less is known about the results of the routine thought reform practiced on the general population. Official statements have repeatedly noted that "well over 95 percent" of the population "support the socialist system" and should be "united with," and that "less than 5 percent" are hostile to the socialist state and should be reformed. Mao's writings frequently contained these figures and they still appear in today's press. "In conducting investigations," exhorted the *Xinjiang Daily* on October 18, 1977, for example, "it is essential to . . . unite with over 95 percent of the cadres and masses and achieve maximum isolation of the most diehard elements and concentrate our blows on them. In the meantime, it is necessary to deal telling blows at those imperialist rich peasants, counter-revolutionaries, bad elements and rightists who hate socialism."[23] In a population estimated in 1977 to number 982,531,000, this meant that almost 50 million individuals were still in need of reform.

Given the enormity of the task of reforming the values of an entire society and keeping them uncontaminated with rival ideas, these results are, of course, not surprising. The intensive brainwashing imposed on prisoners — often held in isolation, kept on a starvation diet, and subjected to severe psychological stress and strain — is not always successful in breaking recalcitrants, and the far less demanding environment of the small group indoctrination network similarly cannot guarantee the creation of a new man in all instances. The goal of ideological unanimity thus most likely will continue to elude the rulers of Communist China.

Wall posters expressing dissident ideas have appeared from time to time in recent years. In November 1974 three young men in their early thirties penned a wall poster of 77 pages in Canton in which they denounced the Communist party as a corrupt new "privileged stratum" that was governing the country without law or democracy. "We cannot forget the grotesque dance of loyalty, the uninterrupted rituals of loyalty, the morning prayers, the evening confessionals, the meetings, the assemblies, all of it lacquered over with a thick religious sauce giving off a strong smell of God." The authors of this denunciation of the cult of Mao were dragged to 100 public struggle sessions but failed to repent. Five years later the three were released from prison and exonerated at another mass rally.[24] Other oppositionists, taking advantage of the seemingly less restrictive regime of Deng Xiaoping, have not been so fortunate. In a communiqué released following a meeting of the Central Committee of the Communist party held in December 1978, the party criticized the way in which democratic centralism had been implemented in previous years, but at the same time warned against relaxing the class struggle against counterrevolutionary elements or weakening the dictatorship of the proletariat. It also reemphasized the importance of ideological indoctrination: "Leadership at all levels should be good at concentrating the correct ideas of the masses and using explanation and persuasion in dealing with incorrect ideas."[25]

The system of political surveillance meanwhile appears to function more or less as before the death of Mao. Under a criminal code adopted by the National People's Congress, China's nominal legislature, in 1979, no one is supposed to be arrested purely for having "reactionary thoughts" or for being a member of a "reactionary" class; a person must commit a criminal offense to be arrested. But the list of crimes includes any attempt to "overthrow the dictatorship of the proletariat and socialist system" — a very vague provision. In the prisons, too, the regimen is little changed. In July 1979 an American delegation, headed by Secretary of Health, Education, and Welfare, Joseph A. Califano, Jr., was granted the rare privilege of touring a Chinese prison in Shanghai. The prison's chief political commissar explained that after six hours of work in the morning the prisoners in the afternoon participated in political study sessions. Well-thumbed copies of the works of Mao Zedong were available in racks in every cellblock. Special cells with heavy windowless doors and writing tables were set aside for prisoners to compose their confessions, a mandatory act.[26]

Similarly, Vietnamese soldiers captured in the recent war with China were put through the traditional thought reform. Vietnamese enlisted men were kept in groups of eight with one of them appointed as leader; his job was to preside over the daily discussions based on "study materials" dealing with the Chinese-Vietnamese conflict supplied by their captors. These leaders also collected the written statements made by the prisoners. Chinese guards at times were present at these study sessions; political officers offered explanations of the Chinese point of view. At one such Prisoner of War camp, about 70 miles from the Vietnamese border, Chinese officials explained to a visiting American reporter that within less than a month 30 percent of the prisoners had seen the light about Vietnamese aggression and some had even applied for permission to stay in China after the expected repatriation of prisoners.[27]

Chinese thought reform involves an attempt to develop a new set of moral and political standards in an adult person in the place of a superego already formed. The degree of coercion present varies from the dynamics of a small group, with its tendency to exact conformity, to solitary confinement, chains, and beatings. In this way, the previous mental equilibrium of the person is uprooted and a psychological vacuum is created, which can then be filled with new norms and values. The goal is to create a new man with correct attitudes and to overcome the false consciousness of bourgeois society. It remains to be seen whether this ambitious plan to cure the Chinese people of "bad ideas" will succeed.

Notes

1. Cf. Paul Hollander, "Criticism and Self-Criticism," *Marxism, Communism and Western Society: A Comparative Encyclopedia* (New York, 1972), pp. 257–62.
2. Edgar H. Schein, *Coercive Persuasion* (New York, 1961), p. 62.
3. Cited by Robert J. Lifton, *Thought Reform and the Psychology of Totalism: A Study of "Brainwashing" in China* (New York, 1961), p. 390.
4. Mao Tse-tung, "Correcting Unorthodox Tendencies in Learning, the Party, and Literature and Arts," cited by Lifton, op. cit., pp. 13–14.
5. Mao Tse-tung, "Where Do Correct Ideas Come From?" (May 1963), in Mao Tse-tung and Lin Piao, *Post-Revolutionary Writings* (Garden City, N.Y., 1972), p. 267.
6. Theodore H. E. Chen, *Thought Reform of the Chinese Intellectuals* (Hong Kong, 1960), pp. 10–11.

7. Statement by Mao Zedong in a session of the National Committee of the Chinese People's Political Consultation Conference (October 23, 1951), cited by Chen, op. cit., p. 11.
8. Mao Tse-tung, "On the Correct Handling of Contradictions among the People," (February 27, 1957), in *Post-Revolutionary Writings,* pp. 177, 182.
9. Cf. Fox Butterfield, "Peking Indictment Accuses Radicals of Killing 34,000," *New York Times,* November 17, 1980.
10. Peter R. Moody, *Opposition and Dissent in Contemporary China* (Stanford, Calif., 1977), p. 59.
11. Moody, op. cit., p. 58. See also Frederick C. Teiwes, *Politics and Purges in China: Rectification and the Decline of Party Norms 1950–1965* (White Plains, N.Y., 1979), pp. 54–56.
12. Martin King Whyte, *Small Groups and Political Ritual in China* (Berkeley, Calif., 1974), p. 231; Victor H. Li, "Law and Penology: System of Reform and Correction," in Michel Oksenberg, ed., *China's Developmental Experience* (New York, 1973), p. 154.
13. Whyte, op. cit., p. 13.
14. Sidney Leonard Greenblatt, "Campaigns and the Manufacture of Deviance in Chinese Society," in Amy Auerbacher Wilson et al., eds., *Deviance and Social Control in Chinese Society* (New York, 1977), p. 91.
15. See, for example, Harriet Mills, "Thought Reform: Ideological Remolding in China," *Atlantic Monthly* (December, 1959), pp. 71–77.
16. A. Doak Barnett, *Communist China: The Early Years, 1949–55* (New York, 1964), p. 94. There is no evidence to indicate that the basic pattern described here has changed to any significant extent since then.
17. Article 1 of "Act of the People's Republic of China for Reform Through Labour" (1954), quoted in Amnesty International, *Political Imprisonment in the People's Republic of China* (London, 1978), pp. 75–76.
18. Ibid., pp. 137–38.
19. Bao Ruo-wang, *Prisoner of Mao* (Harmondsworth, 1976), pp. 61–62.
20. Ibid., p. 46.
21. Lai Ying, *The Thirty-Sixth Way: A Personal Account of Imprisonment and Escape from Red China,* trans. Edward Behr and Sidney Liu (New York, 1969), p. 128.
22. Allyn and Adele Rickett, *Prisoners of Liberation: Four Years in a Chinese Communist Prison* (Garden City, N.Y., 1973), pp. 326, 341, 344.
23. Quoted in Amnesty International, op. cit., p. 30.
24. Fox Butterfield, "Peking Restores 3 Heroes who Assailed Party in '74," *New York Times,* March 24, 1979.
25. "Chinese Party Statement Sets New Economic Goals and Stresses Public Rights," *New York Times,* December 26, 1978.
26. Fox Butterfield, "Shanghai Jail Holds Fewer 'Reactionaries'," *New York Times,* July 4, 1979.
27. John Fraser, "Hanoi Soldiers Get New Line in China Camp," *New York Times,* March 28, 1979.

CHAPTER 4

Emancipatory Pedagogy in the Federal Republic of Germany

Systematic attempts to free people of false consciousness and instill in them true consciousness have not been limited to communist countries. Today, in the educational system of the Federal Republic of Germany, from elementary school through the university, one can find practices that aim at just such proposed enlightenment, variously called "emancipatory pedagogy," or "critical social science." Some of the practitioners of this philosophy of education are orthodox Marxists; others owe their emancipatory concerns to the neo-Marxist Critical Theory of the Frankfurt school developed by Max Horkheimer and Theodor Adorno and later continued by Jürgen Habermas. The political spectrum is wide and includes communists, noncommunist Marxists, members of what in the 1960s was known as the "New Left," as well as left-of-center liberals.

Theoretical Foundations

The theoretical point of departure is a Marxist analysis of society, which by now has become the conventional wisdom in many university departments. According to Professor Claus Offe, a political scientist at the University of Bielefeld, the state in advanced capitalist societies serves the interests of the capitalist class, but hides its class character with the help of selective activities that claim to serve the common good. Political rule in such societies is class rule that protects itself through "organized concealment" — the institutions of the state reinforce "false consciousness."[1] According to Peter Brückner, until his suspension in 1977 for providing aid to members of the terrorist Baader-Meinhof gang a professor of psychology at the Technische Universität Hannover, the entire process of socialization has a repressive function. Education inculcates loyalty to God and country, the virtues of duty, responsibility, obedience, which are "the idols of false consciousness." Would it not be nice, Brückner asked, "if we could achieve our mutual erotic satisfaction without fear, without the restraints of morality or monogamy, if, following our felt needs, we could play with each other naked?" The fact that we cannot do this confirms the existence of false consciousness.[2]

Many, perhaps most, of the advocates of an emancipatory pedagogy and a critical social science reject Brückner's countercultural beliefs that bear the imprint of the 1960s. But, like Brückner, they insist that it is the task of education to free students from structures that prevent self-determination and hinder true creativity. Education must teach young persons to unmask ideologies, to see through manipulation, and to achieve true autonomy. A critical social science, based on reason, writes Professor Karl-Otto Apel, a philosopher at the University of Frankfurt, must expose institutional alienation and false consciousness.[3] The aim of political education, maintains Professor Rolf Schmiederer, an educationist at the University of Giessen, is the emancipation of man and the democratization of society. Beyond the achievement of human rights, the meaning of emancipation must be derived from a scientific analysis of society, an analysis informed by an emancipatory consciousness.[4]

The followers of the Frankfurt school base their critical approach on the assumption that an autonomous ego (self) and an emancipated society reciprocally require each other.[5] The goal is a rational and humane society without injustice, but society cannot be emancipated without the emancipation of individuals. Brückner, therefore, sees false consciousness created not only by the structures of capitalist society but also by "Stalinist regression."[6] Apel denies that a party elite can embody the "objective interests" of society.[7] Man cannot be enabled to fight for his emancipation, insists Professor Kurt Gerhard Fischer, an educationist at the University of Giessen, through the agency of an educational dictatorship or by being reduced to dependency (*Unmündigkeit*).[8]

All this, of course, leaves unresolved the question of the normative foundation on which the struggle for emancipation and the critique of ideological distortion is to rest. If, as Horkheimer acknowledged, "the idea of a rational organization of society that will meet the needs of the whole community" is "not correctly grasped by individuals or by the common mind," and, if, contrary to the expectations of Marx and Engels, "even the situation of the proletariat is, in this society, no guarantee of correct knowledge,"[9] then the standpoint of the critic of false consciousness is left undefined and unsupported, and this leads to what Alasdair MacIntyre has called "epistemological self-righteousness":

> Claims about hallucination, illusion, distortion of thought, and the like can in general be made only from the standpoint of claims that the contrast can clearly be drawn between the hallucinatory, illusory, or distorted mode of perception or thought, on the one hand, and genuine perceptions of reality or rigorous and undistorted reflection and deliberation on the other. Hence, to identify ideological distortion one must not be a victim of it oneself. The claim to a privileged exemption from such distortion seems to be presupposed when such distortion is identified in others.[10]

This problem does not trouble the more orthodox Marxist, and occasionally communist, educators who ground their critique in the Marxist science of society. Scientific socialism, argues Professor Hans Jorg Sandkühler, a philosopher at the University of Bremen, is a theory of a new type. It combines theory and praxis, considers the coming of a socialist society both necessary and possible, and must insist that it alone represents scientific truth.[11] An awareness of what must and ought to be done can therefore be acquired through a study of political economy, through a correct understanding of the structures and contradictions of bourgeois society. Schools under capitalism inculcate obedience and conformity and thus create false consciousness. " 'Correct consciousness' among pupils," argues Professor Hans-Günter Rolff, an educationist at the Pädagogische Hochschule Dortmund, "can develop only after they have learnt to explain the appearances of capitalism in terms of the essence of the capitalist mode of production and come to know at the same time what objective possibilities exist for human development." Strategic learning will therefore aim at communicating the ability to act strategically — the ability to work for liberation from repression "which means acting against capitalism. Such action is strategic because it seeks to link day-to-day activities to the long-range goal, sets intermediate goals and endeavors, step-by-step, to conquer positions of power."[12]

Heinz-Joachim Heydorn, until his recent death professor of education at the University of Frankfurt, cited Lenin and pointed out that the working class on its own can develop only trade union consciousness. To move it toward revolution there is need for leadership by the educated, and education therefore becomes a powerful lever for social change. "Education is a revolution of consciousness" — the alliance of education and revolution will overcome capitalism.[13] The assertion that emancipation can be achieved by way of educational reforms, argues Professor Johannes Beck, an educationist at the University of Bremen, is an error that benefits the bourgeoisie. Emancipation cannot be attained under capitalism; knowledge must be used for political action. Teachers should therefore learn about political economy, the history of the working-class movement, and the class struggles of the present. Their study must be scientific, based on Marxism, and in this way will promote the emancipation of the masses.[14]

Such instruction cannot be impartial. Bourgeois ideologists, writes Professor Reinhard Kühnl, a political scientist at the University of Marburg, make a fetish of the value-free character of science. "Socialists, on the other hand, propagate partiality. They can do so because they are partial toward the great mass of the people."[15] Scientific teaching, insists Johannes Beck, is based on the real foundations of society, serves the emancipation of the masses, and "is therefore teaching partiality toward the working class." The dominant bourgeois science and pedagogy pretend to communicate value-free factual knowledge while in reality they are partial toward the ruling class.[16] Pedagogy should abandon its false "objectivity," argues Professor Hans-Jochen Gamm, an educationist at the Technische Hochschule Darmstadt, and instead should enable pupils to take their place in the class struggle. The schools should create socialist consciousness even if it takes decades before such education leads to concrete political results.[17]

Gamm sees special possibilities for such consciousness-raising in the vocational schools, attended by a majority of all pupils between the ages of 15 to 18.[18] Rolff and Tillmann suggest that even pupils below the age of 14 can be made to see their real interests.[19] And some educationists favor the setting up of day-care centers "in which children learn to emancipate themselves, take the initiative, think critically and in terms of class struggle," so that they will not accept the dictates of the ruling class as they grow older. In these centers children should be exposed to a new socialist children's literature instead of being brought up on the traditional fairy tales that provide "release in false idyllic fantasies that prevent the development of class and historical consciousness."[20] In order to promote solidarity, teachers at all levels should minimize competition for achievement, refrain from anxiety-inducing examinations and grades, and oppose the system of staying behind.[21]

Since the early 1970s, when many of the books discussed so far were published, there has developed considerable political opposition to the propagation of these teachings, a subject to which we will return. On the other hand, a large number of young people in the 1960s and early 1970s were strongly influenced by these ideas and many of them today occupy teaching positions in the schools and universities of the country, especially in those *Länder* that are governed by the Social Democratic party. For the Social Democrats the introduction of the tripartite system of governance for the universities appeared to be a convenient way to defuse student unrest, and the same effect was expected from the appointment of young, radical teachers. The *Gruppenprinzip* weakened the role of the senior professors in the process of appointments and, at a time of rapidly rising enrollments, this fact, too, facilitated the hiring of radical faculty members whose formal academic credentials often left much to be desired. There exist no statistics on the total number of such radical teachers, but their strong presence, especially in the faculties of the social sciences and humanities, is common knowledge in Germany. Some of the most striking examples of this radical influence will be examined in the following pages.

The University of Bremen

Among the institutions of higher learning where the idea of emancipatory education has taken a dominant hold is the University of Bremen.

This university opened its doors in the fall of 1971 with 400 students, and by 1978 had an enrollment close to 7,000. As the university's first chancellor the Social Democratic administration of Bremen appointed a young professor from the Technische Universität Hannover, Thomas von der Vring, who had studied history and the social sciences at the universities of Munich and Frankfurt. The 33-year-old von der Vring at the time was deputy national chairman of the *Jungsozialisten* (*Jusos*), the youth organization of the German Social Democrats, which is considerably more radical than its parent party. A statement of principles, submitted by von der Vring with his application for the position of chancellor, reflected the influence of the Frankfurt school. Von der Vring proposed that the new university be critical of the social status quo, partial toward social progress, and committed to the interests of the underprivileged. A "progressive university," he argued, should work for the "democratization, equalization and humanization of society." It should be devoted to "enlightenment, the critique and unmasking of reality," its critical scholarship should serve social change.[22]

By appointing von der Vring the city fathers of Bremen indicated their acceptance of these ideas. In a speech before the *Bürgerschaft* (parliament) of Bremen on September 2, 1970, Mayor Hans Koschnick described the new model of a university to be created as one that would promote a critical attitude toward society in both research and teaching. The University of Bremen would be devoted to the creation of "critical consciousness toward the social, political, economic processes of society."[23] Bremen would be a reform university, and that meant, it was clear from the start, that it would endeavor to hire teachers who shared the same values. "The commitment to a progressive reform university," declared the new chancellor in October 1970, "implies a political decision, which restricts the pluralism of political viewpoints at the reform university and creates political one-sidedness."[24]

Radical students initially had demanded the opening of the universities to Marxists and a greater "pluralism of methods," and this demand had been supported by many nonradicals. It is ironic, though hardly surprising, that as soon as these same radicals had won positions of influence they used their new power to restrict or abandon pluralism. According to Professor Wolfgang Brüggemann of Dortmund, a prominent member of the Christian Democratic Union (CDU) and of the legislature of North Rhine-Westphalia, applicants for positions at the University of Bremen until 1974 received the following statement about the scholarship expected from new appointees: "The scholar has to understand society as historically developed, changing and therefore changeable; he must see scholarship not as divorced from material conditions but as a reflection of the contradictions of the capitalist mode of production."[25]

Given these expectations, it is not surprising that the faculty of the University of Bremen is predominantly young (average age below 40 years) and on the Left. It is estimated that about half of the professors are Marxists, ranging from the left wing of the *Jusos* to the Maoist *Kommunistischer Bund Westdeutschland*.[26] In elections to the *Konvent*, the university parliament, in 1977, 122 of 277 teachers voting are reported to have cast their vote for lists of orthodox Marxist and communist groups.[27] According to the present chancellor of the University of Bremen, Alexander Wittkowsky, the high proportion of leftist professors is understandable in view of the commitment of Bremen scholars to the improvement of the situation of the working class.[28]

The commitment of a public institution of learning to the support of the interests of one segment of the population, even a majority, would seem to raise weighty questions of academic ethics: it politicizes university teaching and research. It is one thing for individual scientists at a university to engage in research that promotes agricultural or industrial development, or for an institute within a university to deal exclusively with labor relations or the problems of the handicapped. Land grant institutions in the United States sponsor scientific and technological programs that benefit agricultural or industrial production. None of these activities are welded to a specific political perspective other than the general assumption that education and research can contribute to the greater well-being of society. It is quite another thing when a university embraces the belief that in order to serve the interests of the working class it must, as insisted upon by von der Vring, maintain a fighting stance against conservative forces, against a "society dominated by conservatism," which "not without reason suspects a connection between criticism and revolution."[29] This latter position creates a situation where a state-supported university quite explicitly takes sides in and involves itself in social conflict. The interests of the working class are defined in the terms of the Marxist doctrine of class struggle and it is taken for granted that only Marxist theory and agitation can truly advance these interests. What matters is not what the workers actually want but what they should want. The existence in Bremen of a state-supported university committed to an "emancipatory science" and the "interests of the underprivileged" (concepts that are not self-defining) disrupts the political consensus of a pluralistic society as surely as would that of a university in Bavaria devoted to the propagation of religious or moral renewal.[30]

The way in which the fulfillment of the political mandate of the reform university of Bremen expresses itself in its classrooms is not fully known to outside observers, but enough has been learned to lend credence to the widespread belief that the University of Bremen functions as a *rote Kaderschmiede* ("hatchery of red cadres"). Descriptions of courses of study in the social sciences indeed at times read like the programs of a training school for Marxist party functionaries. For example, all entering students of law, economics, and the social sciences are required to enroll in a two-semester sequence, "Integrated Study of the Social Sciences" (ISES). Course A, "Praxis of Science," aims at familiarizing students with the social determinants and the technical and sociopolitical functions of science. Course B, "Structure of Bourgeois Society," deals with "the basic laws and historical developments" out of which today's society has emerged. The main themes taken up are "(1) The origins of bourgeois society (linked to a discussion of the idealist vs. the materialist conception of history); (2) The mode of functioning of bourgeois society (commodity production, production of surplus value, accumulation); (3) The emergence of political and juridical institutions for the protection of bourgeois rule; (4) Origins of the working-class movement; (5) The development of bourgeois society up to its present phase of state interventionism."[31]

Course B is supplemented by a series of lectures, open to the public, on a subject of current interest. In the spring semester of 1979 the theme chosen was "Family and Status of Women in Bourgeois Society." All but one of the five lecturers were members of the Bremen faculty; the lectures were subsequently published by the university. As the editor of the volume indicated in her introduction, the lectures dealt with various issues from the theoretical perspective of a "materialist analysis" of society.[32] One of the lecturers acknowledged the existence of sexist prejudices, shared by women, in countries that consider themselves socialist, but even she concluded that the full emancipation of women required "the elimination of inhuman relations of production, based solely on considerations of profit and growth," as demanded by "feminist-socialist groups of Marxist orientation."[33]

The troublesome issue here, it should be stressed, is not the offering of courses or lectures that are governed by a Marxist perspective, but rather the intellectually presumptuous claim that Marxism can provide knowledge about "the basic laws of historical development," that it alone is a science of society. This view, quite logically, leads to the de facto elimination of all other theoretical approaches. Officially, the materialist (Marxist) analysis of society is merely one of many theoretical perspectives followed by Bremen scholars. In reality, the acceptance of pluralism is largely fictitious. Professor Manfred Hinz, who teaches law, acknowledged that even pluralism does not mean the acceptance of any and all viewpoints; his statement appears to reflect a widespread view at the University of Bremen: "That which has been overtaken by history has no right to be reborn even under the claim of pluralism."[34]

The monopoly of the Marxist approach can be seen in the study of economics, which, like other subjects at the University of Bremen, is governed by a perspective that is "emancipatory and in the interest of the underprivileged." The point of departure, the official syllabus stresses, is not industrial society as such but capitalist society characterized by the private ownership of the means of production, the profit motive, and the conflict between wage-labor and capital. The study of economics should, according to this statement, lay bare the essential nature, laws, and contradictions of this society, to create solid scientific knowledge that will overcome ideological "theories that merely mask and stabilize the rule of the dominant."[35] "Bourgeois theories," it is argued, have only limited explanatory power for an understanding of capitalist society; they are to be confronted with the historical-materialist analysis of society, Marxian theory, which will drive home to students the necessity of taking sides in the conflict between wage-labor and capital. Such study will prepare them for a professional life that for the most part will be subject to the interests of the ruling groups; it will enable them to articulate "emancipatory interests" and to seek their realization through political action.[36] The fiscal policy of the capitalist state is accordingly to be explained in terms of "the basic structure of capitalist socialization"; discussion should focus on the "illusion of the welfare state"; educational policy and research programs are to be examined in the context of state-monopoly capitalism that is called *Stamokap*; the analysis of international economic ties is to take up "the role of the German Federal Republic in the system of world imperialism."[37]

The "pluralism of standpoints," which is sometimes still invoked to justify the teaching of the University of Bremen, is so narrowly defined that the thesis of a student belonging to the *Kommunistischer Studentenbund*, a Maoist organization, who held a different view of how the interests of the working class ought to be served, was at first rejected; the student was given his degree only after prolonged controversy. The student had criticized the theory of monopoly developed by Professor Jörg Huffschmid, who, according to the calendar of the university, is professor of "the political economy of the German Federal Republic, with special reference to the materialist analysis of socio-economic processes of concentration."[38] Professor Huffschmid is also an active member of the *Deutsche Kommunistische Partei* (DKP), which is oriented toward the Soviet Union and the German Democratic Republic; he was one of that party's candidates for the Parliament of Bremen in the elections of 1979. In his thesis, also published as a pamphlet with a catchy title, the student had attacked Professor Huffschmid as a vulgar Marxist and revisionist whose arguments unmasked him as a defender of the interests of the bourgeoisie. He had called upon all progressive students, truly on the side of the working class, "to beat professors like Huffschmid politically and theoretically and to drive them out of the universities."[39] Some two years later the student finally was granted his diploma with a thesis entitled "The Theory of Monopoly of Professor Huffschmid — An Economic Defense of Taking Over Rather than Destroying the Bourgeois State."[40]

The extent to which students at the University of Bremen come to accept the political ideas of their instructors is difficult to determine. Some of them probably are attracted to Bremen on account of its political orientation, but the majority of the students appear to be as unpolitical as at many other German universities. The percentage of students voting in elections for various governing bodies of the university has been declining steadily. According to official returns, in the summer semester of 1979, 24.5 percent cast their votes for the student council (vs. 70 percent in 1972) and 12.1 percent voted in elections to the university parliament (vs. 73.4 percent in 1972). A clear majority of those who participate in these elections continue to vote for radical candidates, primarily the *Marxistischer Studentenbund Spartakus*, the student organization of the German Communist party, and the *Jusos*. A relative newcomer among the Left is the *Marxistische Gruppe*, which is aggressively critical of all other Marxist organizations: "We of the *Marxistische Gruppe* declare quite openly," a recent leaflet stated, "that the viewpoint of others does not interest us one bit. We know that only he can be right who reads his Marx *correctly*, and quite clearly only we do read correctly."[41] The fact that the majority of students remains inactive in campus politics may be a sign that despite all efforts at indoctrination the attempt to instill in the students of Bremen a Marxist consciousness is not entirely successful.

On the other hand, a majority of the students proceeding to the doctorate appear to be Marxists. In the academic year 1977–78, the University of Bremen awarded 41 doctoral degrees. The abstracts of 32 dissertations have been published and 18 of the 27 abstracts in the fields of law, social science, and literature indicate a theoretical outlook that is "materialist" or "emancipatory." In some dissertations, such as "The Generality of Law: The Questionable Fervor for Justice in the Legal Structure of the Welfare State" or "Judiciary Against Democracy: The Development of Legal Norms by Judges in the Weimar Republic and Since 1945" or "A Materialist Analysis of the Origins and Development of Business Administration as an Independent Discipline Within the Field of Economics," the Marxist perspective is acknowledged in the abstracts. Other dissertations, such as "The Logical Structue of Karl Marx's Theory of Crises" or "Student Revolt and Marxism" deal with Marxism, presumably from a radical standpoint.[42]

The University of a German *Land* has a virtual monopoly on training its future lawyers, judges, and teachers. The domination of the Marxist approach at the University of Bremen therefore is not compensated for by the fact that many other German universities offer a more balanced curriculum. Also, the University of Bremen functions as a stronghold and sanctuary of the militant Left that on occasion enters into the Bremen political scene with acts of violence. For example, during a recent ceremony held to mark West Germany's 25th year of membership in NATO, in which 1,100 recruits to the armed forces swore their allegiance to the state, some 5,000 leftists battled police and physically attacked the recruits. More than 250 riot policemen were injured in clashes outside the stadium where the ceremony took place; one soldier suffered critical burns when a fire bomb exploded in the bus he was riding in, one of five vehicles set ablaze by the rioters. The dignitaries at the ceremony, including Defense Minister Hans Apel, had to be flown into the stadium by helicopter. Demonstrators fired signal flares and firework rockets at the helicopter.[43]

The Free University of Berlin

Another university where emancipatory currents run strongly is the Free University of Berlin. By the late 1970s the wave of violence that had inundated the Free University[44] had subsided, in part because entire departments by then had fallen under the control of Marxist, communist, or "New Left" junior teachers appointed to cope with a greatly enlarged student body. For example, in the Division of Philosophy and Social Sciences (*Fachbereich* 11), the largest in the Free University with more than 5,000 students, all students must enroll for two semesters in a series of basic courses on the subject of "Bourgeois Society and Scientific Knowledge," which are offered by all departments in the division. The department of sociology is the most explicit in acknowledging its emancipatory ideology, though, here as elsewhere, the use of terminology of the social sciences obscures the dormant Marxist categories and ideas. "The study of sociology," states the catalogue of courses, "has the aim to lay bare the structures, laws, and patterns of rule governing society and to test their legitimacy in order to enable students to contribute to the democratization of all aspects of society."[45]

The Psychological Institute, also part of *Fachbereich* 11, is devoted to the study of "critical psychology," inspired by "critical social theory" and developed in opposition to "bourgeois psychology." In a course entitled "Social-Theoretical Foundations of Psychology/Philosophy and Critique of Political Economy: Being and Consciousness," students study the second and third volumes of Marx's *Das Kapital*, in particular the consciousness of buyers and sellers and of workers and capitalists. The description of a course entitled "The System of Domination of Institutions" speaks of institutions as "stabilizing power relationships and perpetuating the rule of man over man." All the more urgent, therefore, the course description continues, "is the critique of traditional institutions which stand in the way of emancipation."[46]

Even communist students not belonging to the dominant Socialist Unity party of West Berlin (a branch of the Socialist Unity party that rules communist East Germany) decry the oppressive atmosphere at the institute. A member of the Maoist *Kommunistischer Studentenverband* complained in early 1979, probably only partly in jest, that the Psychological Institute proves its bona fide leftist character by making students learn *Das Kapital* by heart.[47] By 1971 tensions among teachers had become so extreme that the administration of the university agreed to a partition of the institute. Since then the Free University has the Psychological Institute, devoted to the study of "critical psychology," and an Institute of Psychology that belongs to the Division of Education (*Fachbereich* 12) and that teaches what its critics deride as "bourgeois psychology." In the Psychological Institute students routinely receive the highest grades; the Institute of Psychology is a demanding place and enjoys a good reputation in the profession.

One of the few recent instances of violent disruption at the Free University took place in April of 1979 at the Otto Suhr Institute of Political Science to protest the appointment of Professor Heinrich Oberreuter. A leaflet issued by an organization of political scientists close to the Socialist Unity party of East Germany (*Aktionsgemeinschaft Demokratischer und Sozialistischer Politologen*) protested the appointment of the allegedly reactionary professor as an affront to "truly democratic scholarship," which is aimed at "promoting the interests of the working people." The leaflet called on students to meet in front of the room where Professor Oberreuter was scheduled to give his first lecture in order to hear a "counter-lecture" on "Theory and Politics of Heinrich Obberreuter." Led by an assistant professor, some 200 students indeed succeeded in this way to prevent Professor Oberreuter from lecturing. The agitation eventually died down, but, boycotted by most students, Professor Oberreuter resigned a year later to accept an appointment at the University of Passau in Bavaria.

A minority faction in the Otto Suhr Institute continues to challenge the domination of the radicals. The hand of the latter can be seen at work in the curriculum of the institute. The offering of the institute abounds in courses that study Marx's *Das Kapital*, the writings of Stalin, German Social Democracy and the trade union movement "as a pillar of the status quo and capitalist democracy." One course offers students the opportunity to participate in the editing of a newsletter, *Anti-militarismus Information*; credit is given for a contribution to the journal and for a report on the sources used.[48] Many of these courses appear to live up to what a *Juso* leaflet against Professor Oberreuter called the function of political science at the Otto Suhr Institute — "to promote a broad-based antifascist consciousness."

In the early 1970s the John F. Kennedy Institute for North American Studies at the Free University was known as the "Institute for Anti-American Studies." When a group of teachers challenged this characterization as libelous, a Berlin court in 1974 found that it was "truthful and appropriate" to call the institute by that name because its courses of study presented a political caricature of the United States.[49] Since then, the Kennedy Institute has become somewhat less political, but no such change has occurred at another West Berlin school, the *Fachhochschule für Wirtschaft*. Founded in 1971, the school is headed by a chancellor, Edgar Uherek, who takes pride in the political mission of his institution. The *Fachhochschule*, the chancellor declared in a report on his first two years in office, cannot merely provide technical instruction that postulates the existing economic system; as a democratic institution it has the obligation "to reflect critically on the basic socioeconomic relations, a subject ignored by mere technical study, and to achieve a raising of consciousness that will encourage change and social progress."[50]

At the *Fachhochschule für Wirtschaft*, the required basic courses were set up to provide "critical knowledge" that would enable students to engage in "emancipatory, innovative conduct."[51] The content of these courses was prescribed and so was the Marxist perspective under which they were to be taught. The study of political economy was to elucidate the conflict between labor and capital, the concepts of alienation, commodity production, surplus value, rate of profit, etc. In September 1975, Professors Grams, Renner, and Weinberg complained to the Berlin senator (minister) for science and art against the imposition of an ideological straightjacket on their teaching, and the senator several times requested a modification of this program of political indoctrination. But as late as 1978 the basic structure of the introductory courses had remained unchanged. Professors unwilling to conform with the prescribed political line were insulted and their lectures disrupted. Because of its reputation as a Marxist *Kaderschmiede*, graduates of the *Fachhochschule* have great difficulty finding employment. The number of students studying at the school over the years has declined steadily and some critics have called for its closing.

The Philipps-University of Marburg

Next to Bremen and Berlin, the influence of Marxist and communist teachers is most pronounced at the Philipps-University of Marburg, especially in the Division of Social Sciences (*Fachbereich* 03), which includes the disciplines of political science, sociology, and philosophy. The division is dominated by teachers belonging to or closely associated with the *Deutsche Kommunistische Partei*, and it attracts like-minded students from all over West Germany. A leaflet of the *Marxistischer Studentenbund Spartakus*, the Communist party's student organization, distributed at the beginning of the fall semester of 1979, explained that the task of students was to understand and change a society that daily corrupted its members. It then asked rhetorically: "At which university in the German

Federal Republic can I do this? In Marburg, in the division of social sciences; for this reason I have come here. . . . The program of basic courses in the social sciences provides us with the scientific postulates for such activity."[52] Or as Professor Reinhard Kühnl, a political scientist, has put it: "When false consciousness is the expression of a false social *praxis* of men, the aim must be to revolutionize this very false *praxis*."[53]

The introductory program of studies in the division consists of three courses that must be taken in sequence: "Introduction to Sociology and the Analysis of Society," "Development of Bourgeois Society," and "Introduction to the Marxian Analysis of Capitalism." In the last few years the minority faction in the division has successfully fought for an arrangement under which these courses are offered by both Marxist-Leninist and non-Marxist teachers, but in consequence of the small number of non-Marxists this is not always possible in practice. In the fall semester of 1979, for example, students had no choice but to take the third of the introductory courses — "The Marxian Analysis of Capitalism" — with Professor Georg Fülberth, a member of the *Deutsche Kommunistische Partei*, whose published writings mark him as a party ideologue faithfully following the party line. Proving his case with quotations from Marx, Lenin, and Ulbricht, Professor Fülberth considers the Western democracies a "dictatorship of the bourgeoisie," while the German Democratic Republic represents a new kind of democracy in which the protection of individual rights has been superseded by "the right to the creative development of the human personality under socialism." The building of the Berlin Wall Professor Fülberth considered necessary in order to protect the German Democratic Republic against "the economic and ideological offensive of the Federal Republic of Germany and other imperialist powers."[54]

In addition to enrolling in these introductory courses, taught by members of the academic staff, students are required to attend a tutorial for each course that is taught by student tutors.[55] As a result of the political power wielded by the *Deutsche Kommunistische Partei* and the *Marxistische Studentenbund Spartakus* in the governance of the division, the great majority of these tutors are communist activists who, as one observer put it, "see to it that the newcomers receive the 'correct consciousness.' "[56] Even members of other Marxist groups — Trotzkyists and Maoists — are generally excluded from appointments as tutors. Many students complain about the crude propaganda that occurs in these tutorials.

The development of the University of Marburg into what some today call a *Parteihochschule* (Communist party college) is in part a product of the influence of the political scientist Professor Wolfgang Abendroth, a Marxist scholar of considerable reputation, a long-time member of the Social Democratic party, and originally very critical of the German communists; he left East Germany because of these ideological differences.

Professor Abendroth was a charismatic teacher who quite explicitly rejected the distinction between scientific statements and political arguments. Over his long years of teaching he developed a large following not only among students of political science but also among those studying German and English language and literature, education, and theology. Many of his students subsequently became members of the teaching staff in their respective disciplines at Marburg. During the days of the student revolt, Professor Abendroth developed a strong influence on the *Sozialistische Deutsche Studentenbund* (SDS). In the late 1960s Abendroth moved closer to the *Deutsche Kommunistische Partei*, which led to his expulsion from the Social Democratic party, and many of his pupils moved leftward with him. Still, as long as Professor Abendroth taught at Marburg, there prevailed a certain Marxist pluralism. This pluralism disappeared almost completely in the 1970s; today there exists a minority faction that occasionally wins a battle with the dominant *Deutsche Kommunistische Partei*. Convinced that the Social Democratic government of Hesse will have neither the will nor the ability to reverse the politicization and climate of indoctrination at the university, many reputable professors over the last few years have left the University of Marburg. Most of them, like the internationally known historian Professor Ernst Nolte, have made public their letters of resignation in which they decried the intellectual decline of the university.[57]

The Johann Wolfgang Goethe-University of Frankfurt

In February 1923 the *Institut für Sozialforschung* was established at the University of Frankfurt. The original idea of calling it the *Institut für Marxismus* was abandoned as too provocative, but despite a certain pluralism of approaches the members of the institute indeed were Marxists. Following the Nazi assumption of power and the defeat of the socialist working-class movement signified by this event, the intellectual founders of the institute, Horkheimer and Adorno and later Herbert Marcuse, began a reassessment of Marxist doctrine that was eventually to lead to an eclectic neo-Marxism known as "critical theory." When the institute returned from America to Frankfurt in 1950 its distinct intellectual orientation began to be referred to as the "Frankfurt school."

Back in Germany, Horkheimer and Adorno soon developed a considerable following and, together with the writings of Marcuse who had remained in the United States, the teachings of these two men provided many of the main ideas taken up by the "New Left" of the 1960s. It was in Frankfurt that Horkheimer and Adorno had their triumphant hours, only later to be vilified as bourgeois ideologists by radical students of the later 1960s.

Many of the radical professors who later took up the teaching of "emancipatory pedagogy" and "critical social theory" in various German universities were students of Horkheimer and Adorno. Some of the best known of these disciples are Jürgen Habermas, Alfred Schmidt, Oskar Negt, and Albrecht Wellmer. Not surprisingly, to this day Marxists of various kinds dominate the teaching of the social sciences at the University of Frankfurt. According to a mimeographed introduction to the social sciences, drawn up in 1975 for an obligatory short course for beginning students, only a "critical-materialist theory" is able to understand the existing capitalist society, its basic structures, and the laws of its development. Such a critical social science considers "the abolition of the capitalist class society not only as desirable, but, as a result of the scientific analysis of social contradictions, as possible and necessary." The central purpose of the study of the social sciences, therefore, is the acquisition of knowledge that will prepare students to play an active political role in capitalist society with the goal of changing it into a community without conflict, a community without rulers and oppressed.[58]

Some teachers belonging to the non-Marxist minority of the division used this introduction in order to demonstrate the simplistic nature of this Marxist approach to the social sciences. Others ignored it entirely. But to this day, the majority of the courses offered have an outright Marxist or neo-Marxist perspective. As at other universities where the teaching of "critical consciousness" is in vogue, the terminology employed in the description of these courses is often vague and pretentious. The enthusiasm for abstract theory (*Theoriefreudigkeit*), traditional in German scholarship, seems to have received a new lease on life through the critical theory of the Frankfurt school. It is a paradoxical fact, Professor Kurt Sontheimer has observed, that "a theory aimed at completing the great work of enlightenment has become a kind of secret language, which ignores the need for intelligibility and often also for grammatical and linguistic rationality."[59]

Intellectual Consequences

Other institutions predominantly dedicated to an "emancipatory" role are the new universities of Kassel and Oldenburg. At most other universities the influence of Marxist radicals is less pronounced, and, according to some German observers, there are some institutions that would not appoint anyone suspected of Marxist leanings. Moreover, striking differences often exist within the same university. Marxist, neo-Marxist, and "New Left" teachers and courses taught according to these ideological precepts are generally highly visible in departments of education, sociology, political science, German language and literature, and Protestant theology; the faculties of the natural sciences generally operate along traditional lines. Courses in "political economy," given to a chapter-by-chapter analysis of *Das Kapital* and sometimes lasting several semesters, can be found in the most unlikely humanistic departments. This tendency toward what some call a "seminar Marxism"[60] has created a new kind of sterile scholasticism. The spectacle of thousands of apprentice-political scientists, sociologists, economists, philosophers, and school teachers spending entire terms on *Das Kapital* is sad not because it is an unimportant book or a subversive tract but because this lengthy preoccupation with holy writ necessarily goes at the expense of acquiring important methodological techniques and other substantive knowledge of their subject.

German intellectuals, one Marxist writer reports, today are no longer automatically "subservient and obsequious to the ruling class" and they have made important advances in higher education in particular. "This accounts for the 'repressive tolerance' at the university allowing Marxists to make inroads in the education process."[61] Many of those who in the 1960s protested against the professorial oligarchy today are themselves professors and use their new power to impose a dogmatic ideology and to create positions of strength by appointing teachers who share their political beliefs. The confident manner in which this goal of building an ideological following at times is pursued is illustrated by an advertisement for a new teaching position at the *Fachhochschule* Wiesbaden. The desired field of expertise was described as "Psychology and Social Psychology of Domination and Solidarity." Applicants were to be able to cover subfields such as "Critique of Bourgeois Psychology," "Conditions and Possibilities of Liberation from Bourgeois Privatism," and "Occupational Possibilities of Solidarity with the Dominated: The members of the lower classes and the underclass, the handicapped, the mentally disturbed, children."[62]

The program of "enlightenment" and of "raising of consciousness" is accompanied by a lowering of levels of intellectual performance. Because of the decline of standards in German secondary schools and the partial abolition of formal entrance requirements, many of today's West German university students come to the university ill-prepared. They feel insecure about their ability to succeed and the agitation of segments of the Left against "pressure for achievement" (*Leistungsdruck*) therefore falls on fertile soil. Posters and leaflets issued by various radical student organizations constantly emphasize this theme. A wall inscription in the building housing the Division of Philosophy and Social Sciences of the Free University of Berlin seen by this observer read: "Dogs, do you want to be diligent forever?" A leaflet issued by the *Kommunistischer Studentenbund* at the University of Bremen protested: "The bourgeois state seeks to drive us into the competition of 'each against all.'" The visitor is struck by the ubiquitous presence of the issue of *Leistungsdruck*, which appears to rank among the most important concerns of students at practically all universities. Strikes have been called and won against the introduction of new, more stringent rules for examinations or against regulations limiting the permitted time of study before final examinations have to be taken.

At many universities students are allowed to present "team papers" or take examinations as teams. The requirement that in such cases of "collective academic achievements" (*Gruppenleistungen*) the teachers must ascertain the specific contribution of individual students has often become a dead letter. At "progressive" universities like Berlin, Marburg, and Frankfurt many radical professors consider grades as repressive and they connive at the flouting of standards. A mimeographed introduction to the study of the social sciences given beginning students at the University of Frankfurt encouraged students to cooperate with each other and, after decrying the obstructive role of the central university administration, proposed: The entire issue of how to cope with the problem of "*Leistungsdruck*, etc., should preferably be discussed orally instead of on paper."[63] A manual for new students, prepared by a teacher at the Otto Suhr Institute of Political Science at the Free University of Berlin, advised students to form small study groups and to minimize competition by agreeing on a maximum number of pages in the writing of examinations and theses.[64] As a result of the introduction of "examination democracy," the rate of failure at the Free University fell from 31 percent in 1964 to 2 percent in 1971 among economists, and from 25 percent to 3 percent among students of education.[65] Since then, and as a result of greater emphasis on academic performance, the rate of failure has again risen, but it is still below that of 1963. Grade inflation continues to be an acute problem.[66]

At the University of Bremen teachers and students of each course must decide jointly at the beginning of the semester what oral or written work will be required of students.[67] In a mathematics course for students of electronics in the fall semester of 1978, the 25 participants decided unanimously that successful completion of the course would be demonstrated through exercises and reports rather than examinations, and that the lowest grade would be "good." On the other hand, in courses taught by professors insisting on performance the rule that students and instructors agree on course requirements can lead to lengthy disputes; one such conflict in the same semester paralyzed a physics course for two months. In many instances, formal examinations have been abolished at the University of Bremen and hardly anyone fails. Official figures for the academic year 1978 show a failure rate of 1.5 percent; at the *Fachhochschulen* (technical colleges) of Bremen the rate of failure was 4.8 percent.[68] A similar disparity is revealed when one compares the rate of failure in teacher examinations in Bremen and the rest of the country. In Bremen 0.4 percent failed this examination as against an average of 12.3 percent in the other states of the Federal Republic.[69] Graduates of the University of Bremen are said to have difficulties in being accepted as teachers in the other *Länder*.

The senator (minister) for science and art for the state of Bremen, Horst-Werner Franke, conceded in 1977 that the reputation of the university suffered because many of its professors "regarded grades and examinations repressive measures of the capitalist state that had to be countered in the interest of the emancipation of the oppressed." This was done by avoiding bad grades. Graduates of the university, the senator concluded, who already faced diminished opportunities for employment, would be severely handicapped unless this practice were changed.[70] Indicative of the problems facing graduates of the University of Bremen was the case of a student of psychology in January 1980, who, equipped with a preliminary diploma (*Vordiplom*) achieved without oral or written examinations, was rejected by the University of Frankfurt. A new set of examination rules for the University of Bremen has been under consideration, but it will take more than a change in regulations to end this self-defeating practice.

The Influence of Radicalism in the Universities upon Primary and Secondary Schools

Most schools of education in Germany today have been or are in the process of being integrated into the university system, and the universities now train most of the teachers for primary and secondary schools. Not surprisingly, therefore, the ideas of "emancipatory education" and "critical social science" have percolated from university departments of education down to the primary and secondary schools. As we will see in more detail below, university professors, sympathetic to the neo-Marxism of the Frankfurt school, have had a prominent role in drawing up new curricula and writing textbooks for these schools. Some of these teachers accepted positions in ministries of education and in this way helped shape the content of education.

In the past, German education was often criticized as being excessively authoritarian. The curriculum and standards of discipline were said to be too rigid. Following the downfall of the Third Reich, German educators therefore endeavored to "democratize" the system of public education. Under the influence of American pedagogical ideas of progressive education there emerged a new emphasis on the goals of education rather than on the specific content of courses, an orientation toward the future rather than the past. Many teachers saw themselves as social engineers who would help create a new, more humane individual and society. Greater equality of opportunity and the creation of comprehensive high schools (*Gesamtschulen*) in the place of the old *Gymnasium*, regarded as unduly elitist, were much discussed issues. All this had a special appeal for the

Left, and by the late 1960s educational officials in the states of Hesse and North Rhine-Westphalia, governed by the Social Democrats, began to develop plans for applying the ideas of "emancipatory pedagogy" to primary and secondary education.

A central figure in the creation of a new kind of emancipatory education in Hesse was the minister of education, Professor Ludwig von Friedeburg, a sociologist at the University of Frankfurt and a disciple of Horkheimer and Adorno. In 1968 Professor von Friedeburg convened a commission of teachers and educationists who were given the mandate to review the existing curricula and to propose new educational goals. Following a reorganization of this commission in 1970 into several task forces, the first principles of instruction (*Richtlinien*) were issued in the fall of 1972 and teachers were given the opportunity to try them in the classroom. Final approval was to await the results of a voluntary trial period and the receipt of comments from schools and parents' associations.

Reaction was not slow in coming, with the greatest controversy arising in connection with the principles for social studies and German. As critics pointed out, the picture of society communicated to 10- to 11-year-old pupils was one of inevitable conflict between different interest groups in which students were to find their place. They were to be prepared "for a rational evaluation of existing social conditions," to be enabled to strive for the elimination of inequalities and for "a realization of democracy in all aspects of society."[71] The existing democratic system was derogated as providing merely "formally democratic elections." Students were to be encouraged to ascertain whether in certain situations the need might not arise "temporarily to suspend formally democratic rules and rights in order to protect or improve democratic conditions."[72] Coming at a time when radical students were disrupting universities and engaging in various other forms of violent action, this counsel was read as an open encouragement of illegal conduct. The fact that the suggested comparison between the social orders of the Federal Republic of Germany and the German Democratic Republic was devoid of any elucidation of the meaning of communism or totalitarianism, and that both the Russian invasion of Czechoslovakia and the American war in Vietnam were characterized as "military actions for the preservation of the *status quo*,"[73] strengthened concern about the political bias of these principles.

The endeavor to overcome "domination" and "ideological manipulation" was even more pronounced in the principles for instruction in German. Standard educated speech (*Hochsprache*) was described as a means of stabilizing a stratified society marked by conflict and contradictions; an emphasis on this language would alienate pupils from their social origin. A stress on correct spelling, too, served to subject pupils to the dominant norms. Instead of an introduction to a national canon of great literary works, the principles suggested that students be taught to handle various kinds of "texts." The difference between newspapers or comic strips and literature was minimized. The important thing was to determine the ideological content of a text (Whose interests are promoted? From which questions is attention diverted?) and to discuss its "emancipatory possibilities."[74]

The strong criticism of the guidelines for social studies led to the issue of a revised version in 1973 that toned down some of the most controversial formulations. Instead of "formally democratic" elections, rules, and rights, the second edition spoke of "democratic" elections, rules, and rights; the suspension of democratic rules was entertained not for the improvement of the democratic system but for its protection in case of an emergency (*Notstand*). The comparison between the West and East German social systems now stressed the importance of human rights. Where the first draft had emphasized the need to determine whether the provisions of the West German democratic constitution were indeed being lived up to, the second version acknowledged that the constitution of the Federal Republic was, both in design and reality, the best Germany had ever enjoyed.[75]

At the same time, both critics and defenders of the principles agreed that the basic outlook had remained unchanged. The principles, Professor Thomas Nipperdey, head of the *Institut für Geschichte* of the University of Munich argued, still represented an unacceptable attempt on the part of the state to impose a political dogma: The principles regarded conflict as the key to all social phenomena, sought an end to "domination" and "ideological distortion," and implied that only this "critical" approach could make students aware of their true interests.[76] According to Professor Wolfgang Abendroth, who defended the original version, the basic perspective of the principles had been preserved; as before, the aim was to recognize the interests of the "oppressed" and to achieve "democratization."[77]

In the elections of 1974 the coalition of the Social Democratic and the Free Democratic parties governing Hesse lost about one-quarter of the votes cast for it in 1970. The controversial educational policies of Professor von Friedeburg were blamed for this setback and he was forced to relinquish his post. But this resignation has not ended the political storm. The principles for some subjects are now being used on what is still described as a trial basis. The statewide advisory committee of parents, which according to the constitution of Hesse has to be consulted on important educational policies, eventually went to court in order to block the adoption of the contested guidelines for social studies and German. A new draft of the principles for social studies is now nearing completion. Whether the new version will end the controversy remains to be seen.

Similarly inspired by the critical theory of the Frankfurt school were the principles for instruction in civics issued in April 1973 by the state of

North Rhine-Westphalia, West Germany's most populous *Land* and also governed by the Social Democrats. The principles were designed for the classes 9 and 10 — pupils 14 and 15 years of age — of comprehensive schools. The "processes of socialization," it was stated, could conflict with "the interests of the underprivileged." Social norms therefore had to be subjected to constant rational examination. "Emancipation as a goal of political instruction means to enable young people either freely and autonomously to accept the existing social norms or to reject them and, if the occasion arises, to choose different norms."[78] Pupils should be prepared to critically evaluate "patterns of social coercion and domination" and to learn "techniques of innovation or resistance" in order to oppose those patterns found "unacceptable." They should be able "to see through the ideological background of verbal and nonverbal communications" and to participate in social conflicts. They should learn to work for the realization of their demands even if this leads to punishment. Against such sanctions they should learn to defend themselves with "appropriate measures such as acting with solidarity."[79]

Present-day society, the principles pointed out, restricted individual happiness through the "preventable alienation of man at his place of work," the "manipulation of needs," and "unnecessary claims for domination." Society offered opportunities for happiness that were subjectively perceived as satisfying, such as exaggerated consumption or advantages derived from competition, but which in reality represented "shortened and falsified forms of happiness that blocked spontaneity, creativity, and autonomy." To prepare the way for a society that would make possible these new forms of happiness was one of the tasks of political education.[80]

The questioning of basic democratic norms and the unabashed call for a cultural revolution contained in these principles caused a political uproar that forced the minister of education, Jürgen Girgensohn, to order a hasty revision. The new edition of the principles, issued in 1974, included a new section that dealt with the relationship of political instruction and the constitution. Conflicts, it was stressed, should be fought out in a manner that conformed to basic legal norms. Resistance was to be limited to resistance that was "democratically legitimate"; the realization of demands was to be achieved "according to democratic rules."[81] Still, as critics were quick to point out, these changes were superficial. They did not do away with the exaggerated emphasis on social conflict and the simplistic praise of "emancipation" and "social change." The general effect, wrote Professor Joachim Wiesner, a political scientist, was still to relativize the value of individual liberty and to urge students to work for structural changes in their society.[82] While the advocates of these ideas had a perfect right to press for the adoption of such a program through the political process, they were not entitled to impose them upon teachers and pupils in state-supported schools as the only correct and rational position.[83]

Instructional materials prepared in the name of the ministries of education in Hesse and North Rhine-Westphalia meanwhile apply the philosophy of the controversial principles. Between 1973 and 1977, teams of teachers at 37 comprehensive schools in Hesse developed and published such materials (*Konkretisierung von Rahmenrichtlinien an Gesamtschulen*); they are being used in many schools despite vigorous criticism of the political bias to be found in some of them.[84] Commercial publishers, too, entered what they regarded as a promising new market and eagerly contracted with progressive educationists and teachers to prepare textbooks that were written in the new emancipatory spirit. As a result of protests from parents, some of these books, which in their early editions were characterized by a pronounced endeavor to change the political beliefs of children, have since been disapproved by state education authorities or have been revised.[85] But many books that continue to be used in the schools of the states of Hesse, North Rhine-Westphalia, Berlin, and Bremen, which are governed by Social Democrats, still are committed to emancipation from "ideology" and "domination."

A case in point are the textbooks for social studies edited by Kurt Gerhard Fischer, a professor of education at the University of Giessen. The third revised edition of his text, *Mensch und Gesellschaft*, published in 1977, eliminated a chapter ("Power Over Other Men Through Property") that had drawn strong criticism, but the basic political ideology, especially the cultivation of doubt about the existing social rules, remains unchanged. A story in the first edition of 1973 that deplored the need to wear clothing in hot weather is omitted, but the very existence of schools is called into question. Schools, it is pointed out, are a recent invention. "Is it not justified to ask why we must have schools? Would it not be much nicer if we could sleep long every day and then do whatever entered our fancy . . .?"[86] In the same spirit of a utopian hunger for a world without compulsion, politics is defined as "the rule of man over man." A section dealing with leisure time quotes from Marx's *Das Kapital* about the "realm of freedom" and the "realm of necessity," and then suggests that 10- and 11-year-old pupils ask themselves: "Where do we stand *today* in regard to the demands of Karl Marx?" The description of the situation of blacks in the United States includes passages from the writings of Malcolm X and leaves the impression, reinforced by the picture of a collapsing black youth in Harlem, that all blacks are oppressed. A list of the dangers that threaten our world includes racism, nationalism, war, and armaments. The neutrality of Sweden and Switzerland is praised, without, of course, any intimation that such a policy of neutrality might encounter difficulties without the military strength of the Western powers. The general theme is that the pupils live in a society that is steadily getting worse in every way and in which there is little hope for improvement. The total critique of everything that exists implies the rightness of ideologies that promise to set everything right once and for all.

A second example is a series of readers for instruction in German entitled *Kritisches Lesen*. A teacher's manual, issued in 1976, describes the purpose of these readers as a contribution to the "greater humanization of society." The schools cannot accomplish this goal alone, but they can point out faults in that which exists and can create an awareness that bad conditions ought to be changed. The critical teaching of literature assumes, states the manual, that a work of literature "mirrors specific social conditions and struggles." Such an understanding will contribute to "the emancipation of pupils."[88]

Among the social relationships that the authors of this reader consider insufficiently democratic are those between parents and children. Pupils in the sixth school year are asked to analyze the meaning of the fourth commandment: For whom was it written? What are its results? The teacher's manual points out that in view of the almost complete dependence of children on parents this issue must be handled with care. Children of this age will seldom have an insight into their "objective situation." At the same time, "it would seem to be possible, by means of the commandment, to bring into their consciousness that which is part of their experience — the different interests of parents and children."[89] Religious beliefs, too, are to be questioned. A prayer to God is printed followed by questions such as: Who speaks here to whom? The teacher's manual proposes that with the help of these questions "it should be made clear that God is an imaginary addressee."[90] Because of these open attempts to loosen family ties and religious beliefs, many parents are up in arms against such "critical reading." A conference on school texts, held in March 1980 by the German parents' organization, the *Deutscher Elternverein*, demanded the rejection of "emancipatory pedagogy," which it blamed for the rising rate of neurotic disorders and suicides among German youths.[91]

Conclusion

The significance and consequences of these developments in German education in the long run are difficult to estimate. There exist no figures on the total number of Marxists and others committed to "emancipatory education" at the various levels of the educational system. No recent statistics can be found on the political views of primary and secondary school and university teachers, and there are few reliable systematic studies of the political outlook of students and pupils. Surveys do show a growing alienation of students from the democratic system. Between 1967 and 1978 the proportion of university students considering the West German constitution as "more and more distorted in a reactionary and authoritarian manner" grew from 15 to 27 percent; those regarding the federal Parliament as "no longer representing the interests of the people" increased from 12 to 21 percent. One-third of the students questioned in 1978 regarded it as legitimate to use violence in order to achieve political goals (8 percent against persons and property, 25 percent against property only).[92] In a survey of university students carried out in 1979, a similar percentage (34.4 percent) regarded West German society as characterized by fundamental clashes of interests that could not be compromised.[93]

It is an open question whether and for how long after leaving the university these students will continue to adhere to such views. In the real world many young persons will probably outgrow ideas considered "in" and "enlightened" in the sheltered environment of the university. On the other hand, a core of devoted radicals of various kinds will undoubtedly enter adult society and start out on what radical students in the 1960s called "The long march through the institutions." Some of them will probably become teachers and they will attempt to pass on their convictions to the next generation. The basic values of pupils, it is true, are remarkably resilient, little affected by instruction in the schools, and changes in their political consciousness — feared by conservatives and hoped for by radicals — are seldom achieved.[94] Yet the full impact of political indoctrination at universities like Bremen, Berlin, and Marburg is only now beginning to be felt. The states with Social Democratic governments, where various kinds of "consciousness-raising" are most widespread, include almost half of West Germany's population. Parents everywhere complain that a growing percentage of teachers hold a quasi-Marxist view of the world. The rash of terrorist kidnappings and killings in the late 1970s, and the ongoing debate over the exclusion of subversives from the civil service, including the schools, through the so-called *Radikalenerlass*, have given the discussion of these issues a new emotional intensity.

The student movement of the 1960s and early 1970s did not succeed in revolutionizing German society. The boom in social criticism that characterized the 1960s is receding in a more conservative political climate for which Germans have coined the term *Tendenzwende*. Yet the radicals did succeed in moving the political beliefs of opinion leaders — journalists, television broadcasters, leaders of political parties — toward the left. Concepts like pluralist democracy, the rule of law, and the welfare state have lost the unequivocally positive value that they had 20 years ago.[95] There prevails more political confusion and greater receptivity for total solutions. In the survey of students carried out by the *Institut für Demoskopie* Allensbach in 1978, only 6 percent of respondents voiced approval of the political system of existing communist states, but 61 percent felt that the idea of communism was good.[96] Some students judge socialist and communist states by their ideological declarations and pretensions while they evaluate democratic societies according to their performance and condemn them for not living up fully to all of their ideals.

Many Germans fear that their young democratic system is not yet firmly anchored in the consciousness of its people, and they point to strong and widespread residues of authoritarian attitudes. The prevalence of such authoritarian beliefs was one of the reasons why many liberal educationists and teachers in the 1960s were attracted to the idea of an emancipatory education. For those who have come of age during the last 15 years or so there may indeed exist a crisis of legitimacy. Agencies such as the *Bundeszentrale für politische Bildung* (Federal Central Office for Political Education) and its counterparts in the *Länder* stress the importance of active citizenship, but, as in other contemporary democracies, many segments of West Germany's system of education no longer promote patriotism and national loyalty. Instead of affirming the values of the past, these schools encourage a questioning attitude, openness to new ideas, and cultural relativism. But in the absence of a firm moral commitment to the basic democratic order and its underlying values, criticism easily becomes negative and destructive. Educated to be critical of the status quo, many members of a generation that has never experienced political oppression or serious want dramatize the shortcomings of the existing society that does not live up to their model of perfection. They dream of the emancipation of man from "domination" and "ideology," and they become alienated and cynical when the rest of German society does not agree with their salvationary aspirations. This may be a genuine danger to German democracy.

Notes

1. Claus Offe, *Strukturprobleme des kapitalistischen Staates: Aufsätze zur politischen Soziologie* (Frankfurt, 1972), pp. 94–95.
2. Johannes Agnoli and Peter Brückner, *Die Transformation der Demokratie* (Berlin, 1967), p. 101.
3. Karl Otto Apel, "Wissenschaft als Emanzipation? Eine Auseinandersetzung mit der Wissenschaftskonzeption der 'Kritischen Theorie,'" *Zeitschrift für Allgemeine Wissenschaftstheorie*, I, 2 (1970): 192.
4. Rolf Schmiederer, "Anmerkungen zur Curriculumentwicklung für den politischen Unterricht," in Bundeszentrale für Politische Bildung, *Curriculum-Entwicklungen zum Lernfeld Politik* (Bonn, 1974), p. 72.
5. Thomas McCarthy, *The Critical Theory of Jürgen Habermas* (London, 1978), p. 333.
6. Agnoli and Brückner, op. cit., p. 93.
7. Apel, op. cit., p. 186.
8. Kurt Gerhard Fischer, ed., *Zum aktuellen Stand der Theorie und Didaktik der Politischen Bildung* (Stuttgart, 1975), p. 183.
9. Max Horkheimer, *Critical Theory: Selected Essays*, trans. Matthew J. O'Connell et al. (New York, 1972), p. 213.

10. Alasdair MacIntyre, "Ideology, Social Science, and Revolution," *Comparative Politics*, V, 3 (April 1973): 322.

11. Hans Jörg Sandkühler, "Wissenschaftlicher Sozialismus und demokratische Vielfalt," in Horst Heimann, ed., *Dialog statt Dogmatismus: Wissenschaftspluralismus und politische Praxis* (Cologne, 1978), pp. 202–4.

12. Hans-Günter Rolff et al., *Strategisches Lernen in der Gesamtschule: Perspektiven der Schulreform* (Reinbek, 1974), pp. 84–85.

13. Heinz-Joachim Heydorn, *Über den Widerspruch von Bildung und Herrschaft* (Frankfurt, 1970), pp. 337, 331.

14. Johannes Beck, *Lernen in der Klassenschule: Untersuchungen über die Praxis* (Reinbek, 1974), pp. 38, 179–80.

15. Reinhard Kühnl, ed., *Geschichte und Ideologie: Kritische Analyse bundesdeutscher Geschichtsbücher* (Reinbek, 1973), p. 244.

16. Beck, op. cit., p. 190.

17. Hans-Jochen Gamm, *Das Elend der spätbürgerlichen Pädagogik* (Munich, 1972), pp. 60–61, 143.

18. Ibid., p. 145.

19. Rolff, op. cit., pp. 93–94.

20. Jack Zipes, "Educating, Miseducating, Re-educating Children: A Report on Attempts to Desocialize the Capitalist Socialization Process in West Germany," *New German Critique*, I, 1 (Winter, 1973): 152.

21. Rolff, op. cit., p. 95; Beck, op. cit., p. 204.

22. Thomas von der Vring, "Theoretische Überlegungen zum Problem der Universitätsgründung" (May 1970), reprinted in a report on his three-and-one-half year chancellorship, *Hochschulreform in Bremen* (Frankfurt, 1975), pp. 253–61.

23. Cited in ibid., p. 18.

24. "Thesen zum Problem des politischen Pluralismus der Universität," October 22, 1970, reprinted in ibid., pp. 262–64.

25. Wolfgang Brüggemann and Lothar Theodor Lemper, *Uni Bremen: Protokoll einer Dienstfahrt* (Cologne, 1979), p. 49.

26. Rainer Nahrendorf, "Bremen: Eine Uni wehrt sich gegen ihren schlechten Ruf," *Handelsblatt*, January 26–27, 1979.

27. Hermann Segnitz, "Vom Umgang mit einer Reform-Universität," *Freiheit der Wissenschaft*, no. 6 (1979): 99.

28. Alexander Wittkowsky, "Hochschulreform als notwendige gesellschaftliche Aufgabe: Eine Erwiderung," *Materialien zur Hochschul-und Bildungspolitik — Universität Bremen*, no. 2 (1977): 9.

29. Von der Vring, op cit., p. 255.

30. Cf. Richard Löwenthal, *Hochschule für die Demokratie: Grundlinien einer sinnvollen Hochschulreform* (Cologne, 1971), p. 51.

31. Universität Bremen, *Studienführer* (1978/79), pp. 182–83; Barbara Herzbruch and Rudolf Hickel, eds., *Voraussetzungen und Inhalt projektorientierter Ökonomieausbildung in Bremen: Eine Materialsammlung*, 2nd ed. (Bremen, 1977), pp. 435–36.

32. Marlis Krüger, ed., *Familie und Stellung der Frau in der bürgerlichen Gesellschaft* (Bremen, 1979), p. 2.

33. Petra Milhofer, "Rolle der Frau und Familie," in ibid., pp. 28–29.

34. Quoted by Kurt Reumann, "Die Politisierte Universität: Das Bremen Modell und die Arbeiterkammer," *Frankfurter Allgemeine Zeitung*, June 28, 1975.

35. Studiengangskommission Wirtschaftswissenschaft, "Schwerpunkte im Studiengang Wirtschaftswissenschaft," in Herzbruch and Hickel, op. cit., pp. 406–8.
36. Ibid., p. 417.
37. Ibid., pp. 422–28.
38. Universität Bremen, *Hochschullehrerverzeichnis — Veranstaltungsverzeichnis Winter Semester 1979/80*, p. 90.
39. Bernd Hesse, *Die ausserordentlich attraktive Vulgarökonomie des Professor Huffschmid über Spaltung und Mitbestimmung zur Herrschaft einer bürokratischen Monopolbourgeoisie neuen Typs* (Bremen, 1977), p. 68.
40. "Bernd Hesse hat sein Diplom," *Kommunistische Volkszeitung*, February 26, 1979, p. 2. On the entire controversy see also Kommunistischer Studentenbund Bremen-Unterweser, *Dokumentation zur Unterdrückung der Examensarbeit von Bernd Hesse* (Bremen, 1978).
41. Quoted in Felix Semmelroth, "Wozu diese dummen Fragen, Genossen?" *Kursbuch*, 55 (March 1979): 100.
42. *Diskurs: Bremer Beiträge zu Wissenschaft und Gesellschaft*, no. 1 (September 1979): 175–208; see also the list of dissertations in Unversität Bremen, *Forschungsbericht*, 2 (May 1979): 279–90, which shows the same pattern.
43. *New York Times*, May 8, 1980.
44. See Jürgen Domes and Armin Paul Frank, "The Tribulations of the Free University of Berlin," *Minerva*, XIII, 2 (Summer 1975): 183–99.
45. FU Berlin, FB 11, *Kommentiertes Vorlesungsverzeichnis WS 1979/80*, p. 28.
46. Courses 11010 and 11040, ibid., pp. 2, 5.
47. "Linker Konsens am PI — die ADSen und der FB 11," *KSV Arbeitsmaterial*, Berlin region, no. 5 (February, 1979): IV.
48. FU Berlin, FB 15, Politische Wissenschaft, *Kommentiertes Vorlesungsverzeichnis WS 1979/80*, p. 134.
49. Domes and Frank, op. cit., pp. 198–99.
50. Fachhochschule für Wirtschaft, *Erster Rechenschaftsbericht, 1. April 1971 bis 28. März 1973, vorgelegt vom Rektor* (Berlin, 1973) p. VII.
51. See *FHW-Info* no. 2 (March 24, 1975).
52. Leaflet of Marxistischer Studentenbund Spartakus, Gruppe 03, pp. 1–2.
53. Kühnl, op. cit., p. 218.
54. Georg Fülberth and Helge Knüppel, "Bürgerliche und sozialistische Demokratie," in Anne Hartmann et al., *BRD-DDR: Vergleich der Gesellschaftsysteme*, 6th ed. (Cologne, 1977), pp. 212, 241.
55. Philipps-Universität Marburg, Fachbereich Gesellschaftswissenschaften, *Kommentiertes Vorlesungsverzeichnis, WS 79/80*, pp. 1–2.
56. Wilhelm Nikolai Luther, "Vom Missbrauch der Politischen Wissenschaft: Marxistisch-Leninistisches an der Universität Marburg," *Die Politische Meinung*, XXI, 167 (July–August 1976): 85.
57. Cf. CDU Hessen, *Dokumentation: Professorenflucht aus Hessen* (Gelbe Reihe, no. 11; n.p., n.d.). See also Hochschulverband, *Bilanz einer Universität: Denkschrift zum 450 jährigen Bestehen der Philipps-Universität zu Marburg* (Osnabrück, 1977).
58. Universität Frankfurt, Fachbereich 3: Gesellschaftswissenschaften, "Materialien: Orientierungsveranstaltung WS 1975/76," pp. 4, 17–18.
59. Kurt Sontheimer, "Die Sprache linker Theorie," in Wolfgang Bergsdorf, ed., *Wörter als Waffen: Sprache als Mittel der Politik* (Stuttgart, 1979), p. 53.

60. The term "seminar Marxism" at times is also used by dogmatic Marxist activists to characterize critical reinterpretations of Marxism by academic theorists.
61. Zipes, op. cit., p. 157.
62. *Die Zeit*, July 16, 1976.
63. See above, n. 58, p. 15.
64. Wolf Wagner, *Uni-Angst und Uni-Bluff: Wie studieren und sich nicht verlieren* (Berlin, 1977), p. 102.
65. Walter Rüegg, "The Intellectual Situation in German Higher Education," *Minerva*, XIII, 1 (Spring 1975): 110, n. 12.
66. "An der FU hagelt es 'Einsen': Noteninflation in vielen Fächern bei den hochschulinternen Abschlussprüfungen," *Tagesspiegel*, May 25, 1980.
67. Universität Bremen, *Studienführer (1978/79)*, pp. 309, 333.
68. "Weniger Ausfälle bei Schlussexamen," *Bremer Universitäts-Zeitung*, VII, 13 (June 28, 1979).
69. *Freiheit der Wissenschaft*, no. 6 (1979): 96. The figures do not include Hesse and Schleswig-Holstein.
70. Letter of Horst Werner Franke to Hochschullehrergruppe Bremer Modell, June 6, 1977, reprinted in *Freiheit der Wissenschaft*, no. 12 (1978): 9.
71. Der Hessische Kultusminister, *Rahmenrichtlinien Sekundarstufe I: Gesellschaftslehre* (n.p., n.d.), pp. 7, 9, 21.
72. Ibid., pp. 201–2.
73. Ibid., pp. 304–6, 295.
74. Der Hessische Kultusminister, *Rahmenrichtlinien Sekundarstufe I: Deutsch* (Frankfurt, 1972), p. 46 and *passim*.
75. Der Hessische Kultusminister, *Rahmenrichtlinien Sekundarstufe I: Gesellschaftslehre 1973* (Frankfurt, 1973), pp. 270–71, 407–9, 5.
76. Thomas Nipperdey, *Konflikt — Einzige Wahrheit der Gesellschaft? Zur Kritik der hessischen Rahmenrichtlinien* (Osnabrück, 1974), pp. 116–51.
77. Wolfgang Abendroth et al., *Entmündigung statt Aufklärung: Die konservative Kritik an den hessischen Rahmenrichtlinien* (n.p., 1974), p. 43.
78. Der Kultusminister des Landes Nordrhein-Westfalen, *Richtlinien für den Politischen Unterricht* (Düsseldorf, 1973), p. 7.
79. Ibid., pp. 10–11, 13–14.
80. Ibid., p. 19.
81. Der Kultusminister des Landes Nordrhein-Westfalen, *Richtlinien für den Politik-Unterricht* (Stuttgart, 1974), pp. 26, 33.
82. Joachim Wiesner, *Gesellschaft — Staat — Persönlichkeit und Freiheit* (Bonn, n.d.), pp. 17, 34.
83. Clemens and Rudolf Willeke, in Wolfgang Brüggemann, ed., *Bildung oder Indoktrination? Richtlinien für den politischen Unterricht in NRW* (Recklinghausen, 1974), p. 64.
84. See Irene Oswald, "Hurra, keine Freie Welt! Wie hessische Modellversuche in den Schulen für den Sozialismus agitieren," *Frankfurter Allgemeine Zeitung*, September 26, 1978.
85. For some examples see Helmut Schoeck, *Schülermanipulation* (Freiburg/Br., 1976).
86. Kurt Gerhard Fischer et al., *Mensch und Gesellschaft*, 3rd rev. ed. (Stuttgart, 1977), p. 32.
87. Ibid., pp. 11, 239.

88. Hermann Cordes et al., *Lehrerheft* to *Kritisches Lesen 1: Lesebuch für das 5. Schuljahr*, 2nd rev. ed. (Frankfurt, 1976), pp. 5–11.
89. Hermann Cordes et al., *Lehrerheft* to *Kritisches Lesen 2: Lesebuch für das 6. Schuljahr* (Frankfurt, 1975), p. 43.
90. Ibid., p. 44.
91. *General-Anzeiger* (Bonn), March 10, 1980.
92. These results are part of a survey of 500 students at 33 universities and technical colleges in early 1978 carried out by the Allensbach Public Opinion Institute. See Elisabeth Noelle-Neumann, "Wie demokratisch sind unsere Studenten?" *Frankfurter Allgemeine Zeitung*, October 2, 1978. For a critical discussion of this survey see John Tagliabue, "West German Students: Anti-Democratic and Prone to Violence?" *The Chronicle of Higher Education*, XVII, 12 (November 20, 1978), p. 3.
93. This survey was made by the Hochschul-Informations-System and was reported by the *Weser-Kurier*, January 23, 1980.
94. Cf. Erwin K. Scheuch, "Vorbereitung für's Leben? Vom Zustand des Bildungssystems und der Jugend in der Bundesrepublik," in Walter-Raymond Stiftung, *Bildung und Beruf* (Cologne, 1979), pp. 153–54.
95. Kurt Sontheimer, *Das Elend unserer Intellektuellen: Linke Theorie in der Bundesrepublik Deutschland* (Hamburg, 1976), p. 63.
96. See Noelle-Neumann, op. cit.

PART III

**Are Democracy and Capitalism Sustained
by False Consciousness?**

CHAPTER 5

The Case for the Cultural Hegemony of the Dominant Classes

The failure of the working class in the developed countries to rise up against the capitalist system has given the idea of false consciousness new currency. The New Left, in particular, has argued that the ruling classes maintain themselves in power as a result of what the Italian Marxist Antonio Gramsci had called their "cultural hegemony," especially through control of the system of education and the media of communication. In this way the rulers gain the "consent and acquiescence"[1] of the subordinate groups; they remain dominant by creating in the latter false consciousness. The elites of capitalist society, writes the political scientist Michael Parenti, win the empowering responses of the many through a variety of socializing techniques, by keeping tight control over society's values, symbols, and the flow of information. Culture thus becomes "a vital instrument of class power."[2]

As we have seen in an earlier chapter, the central core of this argument had already been developed by Marx and Engels. They, too, had spoken of the capitalist control of "the means of mental production." Yet it was the firm conviction of the founders of scientific socialism that the proletariat eventually would overcome this handicap. Capitalism produces its own gravedigger, the proletariat, wrote Marx in *Das Kapital*, "a class always increasing in numbers, and disciplined, united, organized by the very mechanism of the process of capitalist production itself." The growing contradictions of the capitalist system would lead to its demise because they created a class-conscious proletariat. Ultimately, the rule of the capitalist exploiters of the working class would be overthrown, "the expropriators are expropriated."[3] When this prophecy failed to come true, the New Left fell back upon the Marxian idea of false consciousness, fostered by the ruling class, albeit without the optimistic prediction by Marx and Engels of the ultimate victory of revolutionary consciousness. Unwilling to rely on the enlightening role of a Leninist vanguard party and without espousing a clear conception of true consciousness, New Left theorists for the most part therefore use the notion of false consciousness as a synonym for "distorted consciousness." Many of them are social scientists, and they want to

71

be regarded as scientists rather than philosophers. Hence, the emphasis is on what they regard as a critical analysis of present-day society and the bias of its processes of socialization rather than on the description and defense of a better, ideal society or on an elucidation of what undistorted consciousness might consist of.

The dominant symbols and values of the ruling groups, writes the sociologist Klaus Mueller, for example, have created an official language, followed daily by the mass media and educational institutions, which represses and inhibits the articulation of conflicts and needs on the part of the subordinate groups. Lower-class children and adults are unable to perceive the objective reasons for their deprived condition and to engage in a critical examination of the social structure in which they are caught.[4] The implicit assumption of this argument, it should be noted, is that social problems such as poverty and lack of educational achievement are due to basic structural faults in our society that could be cured by a radical overhaul of this same society. The direction of change is merely hinted at, and the values informing this harsh critique of present-day society are mentioned only in passing. They apparently include such things as meaningful work, "self-direction and social responsibility" and a rejection of consumerism and of the "domination and repression" of advanced capitalism.[5] The superiority of these values over those of the existing capitalist society is taken for granted. Hence, Mueller can state his case as a "critical social scientist" — critical of the status quo but seemingly merely seeking to overcome distortions of perception and mystification — rather than as a philosopher engaged in normative analysis. Anyone not agreeing with Mueller's indictment of capitalist society is therefore suffering from distorted consciousness.

According to a widespread view among critical social scientists, who often proudly call themselves radical social scientists, agencies of socialization such as schools disseminate the values of the ruling class. The objective of primary and secondary education is "to propagate a devotion to the dominant values of the American system," to encourage an uncritical view of American political and economic institutions.[6] The schools "reinforce deprivation by propagating rationalizations or by avoiding pertinent discussion"; individuals and groups therefore "cannot recognize what is in their interest and that of the population at large."[7] Higher education, so the argument runs, for the most part involves simply "more sophisticated extensions of the same socialization." It provides little encouragement to socially heretical elements, Marxists are purged from the universities, and if students occasionally participate in protest activities it is not because of but despite the education they have received.[8] Scholars and intellectuals function as managers of legitimation; political scientists serve as "high priests of the system, teachers who propound the truths and glories of American democracy to the young and thereby generate and sustain its myth."[9] In sum, the socialization of children in late capitalist society involves "a mystification of the nature of political power. . . . a developing process of false consciousness not of political socialization."[10]

A similar manipulative role, these same radical social scientists argue, is played by the media of communication. The newspapers, radio, and television fortify the current preoccupation with consumerism and leisure and obscure the workers' awareness of his inferior status at work and in society. "The function of the media deflects public attention from political issues and perpetuates the definition of the 'good life' in strictly materialistic terms."[11] The media are tied to the business class and operate as "ideological propagators of capitalist values"; they sell not only products but also a social consciousness and a definition of reality, "instilling the kinds of fears, fantasies, titillations, and discontents that express themselves through the fabricated necessities of compulsive production, joyless consumption, and economic and psychological scarcity."[12] Despite an illusion of diversity, a situation has been created in which indoctrination is no longer recognized as indoctrination.

The British Marxist Ralph Miliband presses for a similar indictment. The mass media are said to foster a climate of conformity by treating views that fall outside the consensus as curious heresies or "irrelevant eccentricities which serious and reasonable people may dismiss as of no consequence." The mass media are both the expression of a system of domination and a means of reinforcing it.

> Impartiality and objectivity, in this sense, stop at the point where political consensus itself ends — and the more radical the dissent, the less impartial and objective the media. On this view it does not seem extravagant to suggest that radio and television in all capitalist countries have been consistently and predominantly agencies of conservative indoctrination and that they have done what they could to inoculate their listeners and viewers against dissident thought. This does not require that all such dissent should be prevented from getting an airing. It only requires that the overwhelming bias of the media should be on the other side. And that requirement has been amply met.[13]

The ideological function of the media, Miliband suggests, is obscured by certain features of cultural life such as the existence of debate and controversy and the absence of state dictation. Yet despite a high degree of independence, publicly owned radio and television, too, fulfill "a conformist rather than a critical role." Controversial views are expressed everywhere; they inspire films, and large publishing houses present them in vast paperback editions. In the 1960s, Miliband notes, publishers in advanced capitalist countries found even Marxism an eminently saleable commodity, and what can be described as "commercial Marxism" occurred on a huge scale. Yet, Miliband insists, all this does not change the basic fact that "the agencies of communication and notably the mass media are, in reality, and the expression of dissident views notwithstanding, a crucial element in the legitimation of capitalist society . . . . the free expression of ideas and opinions *mainly* means the free expression of ideas and opinions which are helpful to the prevailing system of power and privilege."[14]

In all, then, the cultural hegemony of the ruling classes means that the individual in advanced capitalist societies has been socialized into an essentially conservative perspective. Subordinate groups that cannot articulate their interests or perceive social conflicts "have been socialized into compliance, so to speak, [and] they accept the definitions of political reality as offered by dominant groups, classes, and governmental institutions." The suppression from public debate of the existing unequal distribution of power "is equivalent to manipulated, thus dictated, communication."[15] Elite control of the socialization process, it is conceded, is not absolute, and it does not equal the rigid control of educational institutions and of the media found in totalitarian systems such as Nazi Germany and the Soviet Union. The ruling elites are not always successful in maintaining their class interests. Yet they succeed often enough in order to confirm the basic character of the system, which remains one of capitalist class rule.

This, very summarily stated, is the case for the proposition that the capitalist mode of production and bourgeois democracy are sustained by the cultural hegemony of the dominant groups who impose false consciousness. In the following two chapters we will subject this position and some of its correlatives to a detailed critique by examining how well it describes America's system of education and its media of communication.

Notes

1. Antonio Gramsci, *Selections from the Prison Notebooks*, ed. Quintin Hoare and G. Nowell Smith (London, 1971), p. 189.
2. Michael Parenti, *Power and the Powerless* (New York, 1978), pp. 216–217.
3. Karl Marx, *Capital: A Critical Analysis of Capitalist Production*, vol. I (Moscow, 1954), p. 763.
4. Klaus Mueller, *The Politics of Communication: A Study in the Political Sociology of Language, Socialization and Legitimation* (New York, 1973), pp. 71, 69, 55.
5. Ibid., pp. 178–79.
6. Parenti, op. cit., pp. 117–18.
7. Mueller, op. cit., p. 23.
8. Parenti, op. cit., pp. 159–62.
9. H. Mark Roelofs, *Ideology and Myth in American Politics: A Critique of a National Political Mind* (Boston, 1976), p. 150.
10. Alan Wolfe, *The Limits of Legitimacy: Political Contradictions of Contemporary Capitalism* (New York, 1977), p. 298.

11. Mueller, op. cit., p. 100.
12. Parenti, op. cit., p. 150.
13. Ralph Miliband, *The State in Capitalist Society* (London, 1969), p. 224.
14. Ibid., p. 220.
15. Mueller, op. cit., pp. 9, 23.

CHAPTER 6

The American System of Education

At the very time when the New Left has pictured the American system of education as serving the interests of the capitalist class, conservative groups — ranging from fundamentalist Christians to the John Birch Society — have accused the schools of fostering atheism, socialism, disrespect for authority, and general immorality. How can the same schools be seen disseminating such different values? The fact that the American system of education has been attacked by both the Left and the Right obviously does not prove that American schools are doing an adequate job, respecting neither orthodoxy nor heterodoxy, but it does draw attention to the complex role played by this important social institution.

Primary and Secondary Schools

In all societies, whatever their political ideology, the schools not only teach certain skills and bodies of knowledge but also transmit to oncoming generations the basic values of the national culture. In America this socializing function of the schools includes the teaching of the principles of self-government — education for democracy — and both defenders and radical critics of American education at times have called this practice "indoctrination." It is the proper business of education, both public and private, wrote the dean of the University of Texas School of Education in 1941, "to imbue young Americans with intelligent devotion to their country's basic principles and ideals. Indoctrination for American democracy is . . . not only a proper, but also a major and necessary, business of American education. It is a plain duty of schools and teachers in this country to give vigorous support to the ideological pattern that sustains them."[1] Education for citizenship in this country, argues Michael Parenti, "replete with flag salutes, national anthem and history books espousing the myths of American virtue and American superiority," is no less indoctrination than the education of children in totalitarian states such as Nazi Germany or the Soviet Union.[2] Many radical teachers justify their indoctrination of pupils with the argument that all education is indoctrination and that they merely engage openly in what others do without proper acknowledgment or awareness.

One can readily concede that the education of young children, including the teaching of morality, involves elements of indoctrination in the sense that such youngsters are taught moral principles or are made to act in certain ways without being given detailed explanations or reasons for doing so. The child must learn basic elements of moral behavior before he can understand them, and it is only much later that a young person, having reached a degree of intellectual maturity and sophistication, will be able to assess critically the ideals and mores, part of his cultural heritage, acquired in his youth. But not all teaching is indoctrination. When students are taught to make valid inferences, to appraise evidence and beliefs by rational means, to detect logical fallacies, to be aware of appeals to authority, and so on, we have education that is the exact opposite of indoctrination. The fact that not all teachers fully live up to these lofty standards of their craft does not eliminate the conceptual distinction between education and indoctrination. As Sidney Hook argues correctly:

> If all teaching entails indoctrination, what would the opposite of indoctrination be? Non-teaching? Ordinary English usage requires a distinction between teaching that indoctrinates and teaching, however rare, that does not. Even if all teachers indoctrinated, it would still be necessary to differentiate conceptually between indoctrination and its absence. Otherwise we could not even identify indoctrination. Even if all men were dishonest, there would still be a conceptual difference in the meanings of "honesty" and "dishonesty."[3]

Not all teaching is identical with indoctrination, and the organization of education in America is such that the indoctrination of all pupils with one world outlook is a practical impossibility. The public school system faces the competition of private and parochial schools, supported and controlled by groups with their own distinctive philosophy of education and committed to diverse political and moral principles. The public schools themselves reveal significant differences, both in terms of the quality of education they provide and its content. Local boards of education often are subjected to outside pressure, but these pressures do not all emanate from one political or ideological source. "Whoever seeks to explain the complicated, overlapping, richly confused patterns of American education in terms of the political or economic interests of a 'power elite,'" writes Sidney Hook, "either misconceives the nature of political power or of an elite or both. For in the medley of forces affecting American education, the influence of Main Street is and has been far more decisive than that of Wall Street."[4]

American public education, as a rule, is committed to the values of democracy, including the particular ideals of the American dream such as the virtues of competition, equality of opportunity, and upward social mobility. The schools also inculcate the importance of discipline, punctuality, and orderly work habits, all of which radical critics consider the result of pressure by vested interests in a capitalist society. Employers need workers who come to work on time and who have orderly habits of work; the schools in a capitalist society therefore teach these essential traits of a capitalist social order. The education system, write Samuel Bowles and Herbert Gintis in their influential book *Schooling in Capitalist America*, is "best understood as an institution which serves to perpetuate the social relationships of economic life through which these patterns are set, by facilitating a smooth integration of youth into the labor force."[5] Indeed, some radical students of American education regard even the teaching of reading as a ploy of the ruling elites. This was the argument, for example, of Neil Postman (who has since changed his mind):

> It is probably true that in a highly complex society, one cannot be governed unless he can read forms, regulations, notices, catalogues, road signs, and the like. Thus, some minimal reading skill is necessary if you are to be a "good citizen," but "good citizen" here means one who can follow the instructions of those who govern him. If you cannot read, you cannot be an obedient citizen. You are also a good citizen if you are an enthusiastic consumer. And so, some minimal reading competence is required if you are going to develop a keen interest in all the products that it is necessary for you to buy. If you do not read, you will be a relatively poor market. In order to be a good and loyal citizen, it is also necessary for you to believe in the myths and superstitions of your society. Therefore, a certain minimal reading skill is needed so that you can learn what these are, or have them reinforced.[6]

There are several problems with this line of thinking. First, and foremost, the teaching of the three Rs and the encouragement of qualities such as punctuality and orderliness may well serve the requirements of a complex, democratic, capitalist society, but is that necessarily and automatically bad? Only those who consider contemporary American society as fundamentally unjust, repressive, and built upon myth will regard the perpetuation of the values of this society as equivalent to the encouragement of false consciousness. American schools, like the schools of all societies, serve as agencies of moral socialization, but to condemn them for doing this job requires more than to point to their having positive functions for being a good citizen or for the performance of adult roles in a capitalist society. Neither, of course, does a *functional* relationship constitute evidence of a *causal* relationship. The fact that certain elites benefit from what the schools teach does not prove that they teach these things *because* the elites want it that way.[7]

Second, radical critics of American public education assume without proof that students do in fact learn what the schools intend to teach them; radicals share this belief with conservative critics. Conservatives are convinced that the schools undermine respect for authority and teach all kinds of "un-American" ideas; radicals are convinced that the schools effectively indoctrinate pupils in the values of capitalism. Both groups believe, as an astute student of contemporary education, Christopher Hurn, has pointed out, that schools are effective in undermining the values they hold dear and ineffective in teaching the things that they would like the schools to teach:

> A reasonable question, of course, is why, if we assume that schools are ineffective in promoting one set of values and purposes, do we assume that they are much more effective in promoting other values and purposes? It may be true that schools are not terribly effective in encouraging students to think for themselves or to challenge existing orthodoxies, but why do we assume that they are much more effective in teaching punctuality and patriotism? Evidence for almost any of these assertions is conspicuously lacking. We simply do not know whether children effectively learn what schools intend to teach them, because we lack an unequivocal way of showing that students learned particular qualities in school rather than at home or in the wider environment outside school.[8]

What little empirical evidence is available on the results of the teaching of civics and social studies, for example, shows that these courses have hardly any discernible impact on the political thinking of pupils. A study undertaken in 1965 of a national sample of high school seniors revealed that their civics curriculum was not significantly associated with the students' political orientation.[9] The same conclusion was reached by two more recent researchers. Whether because these courses are too bland or for other unknown reasons, there is "astonishingly little hard evidence that schools really are important agents of political socialization."[10] As I pointed out in my earlier chapter dealing with West German education, there is so far no clear evidence that the schools are successful in achieving changes in the political consciousness of their students — a result feared by conservatives and hoped for by radicals.

Even if American schools were indeed operating at the behest of certain capitalist elite groups and were set up to train for docility, it would appear that they do a rather poor job. Teachers everywhere complain that their students are undisciplined and rebellious. Ghetto schools report increasing levels of disorder and violence, including armed attacks on teachers and fighting among students. Quite clearly, schools are not very successful in inculcating submissiveness and respect for authority. Schools today not only do not manage to reinforce the values and legitimacy of the capitalist order, but they no longer function as effective agencies of socialization. "What is more and more accurate," concludes Hurn, "is a picture of schools frustrating the objectives of all who seek to use them to convey particular messages to the young: objectives of progressive educators, capitalist elites, parents and local communities."[11]

In a time of unprecedented cultural turmoil and dissent, it is not surprising that the schools of the country have often followed the new currents of opinion. New, more informal methods of teaching and new curricula stress individual initiative and participation and openness to heterodox values and behavior. The more permissive attitudes that came to flourish in the late 1960s and early 1970s have given rise to a host of conservative groups that employ pressure tactics and censorship in order to reestablish the sway of traditional values,[12] but the results of their efforts are mixed. A recent national survey of teachers of social studies found that 80 to 90 percent of them felt free to teach whatever they wanted, and they reported an increased acceptance of the concept of freedom of teaching.[13] Many of the younger teachers, educated during the Vietnam era, are no longer sure what to teach their students about national loyalty and patriotism,[14] the result of widely shared attitudes of political disenchantment. The long-range effects of this situation are yet to be felt.

School textbooks, too, have changed with the times. Bland optimism and chauvinism, Frances FitzGerald reports, have yielded to a preoccupation with problems: "race problems, urban problems, foreign policy problems, problems of pollution, poverty, energy depletion, youthful rebellion, assassinations, and drugs."[15] A study of how the Cold War is treated in six of the most widely used American history textbooks found that the Soviet Union was given a greater benefit of the doubt than the United States was given, reflecting, no doubt, the influence of revisionist historians.[16]

In the face of these many changes in the political character of American public school education, some radical critics have admitted that "though the school system has effectively served the interests of profit and political stability, it has hardly been a finely tuned instrument of manipulation in the hands of socially dominant groups." Along with its socially stabilizing effects, it has also produced an "egalitarian consciousness" and "a powerful radical movement and critique of capitalist society."[17] This admission should not come as a surprise to anyone, for the liberating potential of the massive expansion of formal education and literacy during the last 100 years has been known for a long time. "Teaching a man to read," writes a British scholar, "may make him a pliant consumer and a rote conformist to factory regulations, but it also makes accessible to him the whole of the literature of his mother tongue, including its radical component" — and the writings of Karl Marx (in translation). If the discovery of print puts power into the hands of the literate, then the logic of this fact is that liberation from the tyranny of print can only derive from literacy itself.[18] Spokesmen for the oppressed — from Marx, Lenin, and Gramsci to Paulo Freire — have therefore always emphasized the revolutionary implications of literacy.

The proposition that education in America serves to enhance the social and economic status quo is belied by another set of data. Education, it turns out, does not simply reproduce the existing social order but in fact is a crucial factor contributing to upward mobility. In their study of the American occupational structure, Peter Blau and Otis Dudley Duncan found that the large amount of upward mobility in America was directly related to education — the proportion of men experiencing such mobility increases steadily with the quantity and quality of their schooling.[19] Other studies, including the highly acclaimed work of Christopher Jencks, have confirmed this conclusion. The best observable predictor of how much a person will earn, Jencks found, is the amount of schooling.[20] To be sure, while education is a necessary condition for acquiring the capacity to earn, differences of socioeconomic status continue to differentiate upward mobility by class. Deprived socioeconomic background is not an insurmountable handicap to good school performance, but lack of means does deny some children of the lower classes access to further education. More importantly, the style of upbringing in the home affects those interests and habits of mind that enable the child to profit from education.[21] Still, the fact remains that education continues to matter. The schools are not, as one recent radical critic has charged, "an educational credentialing game . . . rigged to insure that outcomes will be related to class" and reproducing inequality from generation to generation.[22] The advances made by blacks in this country in the last 10 years or so in large measure are related to the opening up of educational opportunity.

That inequalities in school performance in substantial part have their origin in factors operating outside the school, especially the home environment of the child, is now generally recognized. But the link between this early environment and success in school appears to be far more complex than was once believed. The class system, wrote the student of linguistics Basil B. Bernstein in 1974, has had an important effect on the distribution of knowledge. "A tiny percentage of the population has been given access to the principles of intellectual change whereas the rest have been denied such access."[23] The related position of Klaus Mueller that lower-class children and adults suffer from linguistic deficiencies that prevent them from articulating their needs and therefore hold them captive in a social structure they cannot understand has been mentioned in the previous chapter. The "culture of poverty" thesis, made known by the work of Oscar Lewis, has similarly postulated that certain distinct values of this subculture bind successive generations to an impoverished existence. Yet the causal relationship assumed to exist between resignation to poverty and lower educational motivation and achievement involves essentially a tautological or circulatory explanation; other problems arise with similar constructs.

Theories linking impoverished environments to poor school performance and achievement generally are unable to account for the substantial differences among different ethnic groups of similar social status. There is evidence to suggest that success of British working-class boys in secondary schools depends more on the relationship between parent and child than on socioeconomic status.[24] Disagreements over the meaning of IQ further complicate the assessment of the relative importance of various forces in the socialization process. More attention may have to be paid to the child's mental and physical endowment and its evolving cognitive structure, which appear to exert a vital influence on the way in which political stimuli are interpreted and absorbed.[25] In short, at this time available research findings cast doubt on any firm conclusions regarding the effects of deprived class background on educational achievement without, however, giving us an alternative theory integrating all available data. At the very least, therefore, this state of affairs dictates an attitude of caution concerning the often sweeping assertions made by radical critics about American public school education.

Higher Education

If elementary and secondary education in America have begun to reflect new currents of thought and a greater openness to heterodox ideas and values, this situation is even more pronounced in higher education. One measure of this is the fact that college and university teachers are distinctly more liberal in their political outlook than the population at large. Survey data, taken in 1969, for example, reveal the following political self-characterization (the figures represent the percentage of those who identified themselves with a specific political ideology):[26]

	Faculty*	U.S. Public
Left	5	4
Liberal	41	16
Middle-of-the-Road	27	38
Moderately conservative	25	32
Strongly conservative	3	10

*Column adds to 101 because of rounding.

The percentage of left-liberal views was highest in the social sciences and humanities and among the more scholarly and highly achieving faculty; similar findings are reported from Britain and the Federal Republic of Germany. In the 1950s, the presence of a nonconformist maverick like C. Wright Mills at an elite institution like Columbia University was considered a unique demonstration of academic freedom in America. Today the academy holds a sizable community of Marxists and radical teachers; those who complain the loudest that the university is merely a tool of capitalist interests cannot really explain their own presence in it. Seldom, it would seem, has an establishment spent so much money to support its own detractors.

Many college courses today, especially in the social sciences, exhibit an adversary posture toward the operative ideals of American society; the questioning of traditional social institutions and values is often the new orthodoxy. The titles of textbooks and anthologies published for the undergraduate market reflect some of these new currents, and the way in which these books are advertised tells something about the potential audience for this new political conventional wisdom. For example, in 1979, the Bobbs-Merrill Company promoted a book by the radical political scientist Howard Zinn with this description: "Passionate and compassionate, the author leaves no stone standing in his indictment of American imperialism at home and abroad. . . . This American radical conveys new strength and hope in his occasional sightings of the American revolution that is yet to come."[27] The last few years have seen a weakening of the radical impulse on college campuses, but an attitude of general scepticism about many aspects of society and of political cynicism continues to be widespread.

While Marxists and radical college teachers persist in arguing that the colleges and universities of the country are pillars of the social and political status quo, many of them are at the same time busily engaged in using their position in the academy for the purpose of undermining this same status quo. In a recent volume, *Studies in Socialist Pedagogy*, several radical authors openly acknowledge their commitment to political indoctrination. "It is not the accumulation of Marxist knowledge that is our aim for our students (or ourselves)," writes a sociologist, "but the development of revolutionaries, free of bourgeois values" and free from the "false consciousness" from which students suffer.[28] The well-known political scientist Bertell Ollman notes that many obstacles stand in the way of students developing an appreciation of Marxism. The major hurdle "is the bourgeois ideology, the systematic biases and blind spots, which even the most radical bring with them." Also, "the very presence of a Marxist teacher who is allowed to teach Marxism is conclusive evidence to some that bourgeois freedom works — just as students from moderate backgrounds often take their own presence in class and in the university as proof that extensive social mobility and equality of opportunity really exist under capitalism." Nevertheless, Ollman affirms, bourgeois ideology can and must be countered, and Marxism, the science of society and "the only adequate analysis of capitalism today," can be taught successfully. "If non-Marxists see my concern with such questions as an admission that the purpose of my course is to convert students to socialism, I can only answer that in my view — a view that denies the fact-value distinction — a correct understanding of Marxism (or any body of scientific truth) leads automatically to its acceptance."[29] Presumably, therefore, a student who does not agree that Marxism represents a scientific theory of society reveals a faulty understanding of scientific truth and should be graded accordingly.

In a review of this same book, two radical academics note that though the radical thrust of the 1960s seems spent, in reality "radical ideas have spread and deepened. Nowhere is this more true than in the colleges and universities. There are hundreds, perhaps thousands, of openly socialist professors and many more 'fellow travellers.' There is hardly a conventional idea that is not under radical attack." Radical teachers now have an opportunity "to help their students to understand the bourgeois culture which oppresses them, to confront it, and to begin to construct the outlines of a new socialist society." They can get students to abandon their pseudo-values. "Obviously, when only the children of the rich and powerful attended college, radical professors, as teachers, could have no such expectations. . . . Now, however, college teaching itself can be an important radical activity and not simply a way to earn a living."[30]

Radical academics do not deny that they use the classroom for purposes of "consciousness-raising." Among the arguments they use to defend their political proselytizing is the notion that *all* teaching is political and that their approach to the role of the university and instruction is simply more honest than that of their bourgeois critics. To a large extent, the assertion that everything, including teaching, is political involves a platitudinous slogan. Of course, the university is a political institution because it is an integral part of society, because its members — administrators, faculty and students — have economic interests and political biases, because what the university does has political and social consequences. The university is also political in the sense that when it decides to be pluralist and nonpolitical and to oppose its politicization, it makes a political judgment and engages in a political act. But this does not mean that the university is political in the same way that, say, a government agency is an instrument of public policy. Despite all human weaknesses and failings, the world of scholarship and teaching is not identical with the world of politics and its partisans and propagandists. It is only the recognition that we are dealing here with analytically distinct aspects of human conduct that allows us to think about the *proper* relationship between these two spheres.[31]

Another idea used by radical academics in defense of political indoctrination is the denial of the possibility of scientific objectivity, especially in the social sciences. Since everyone is subjective and biased, so the argument seems to run, everyone can be as happily partisan and partial as he likes. This position, it cannot be pointed out too often, is as destructive in practice as it is logically deficient in theory. It is, of course, generally recognized that a scholar may decide to study a certain problem as a result of very different motives — sheer intellectual curiosity or, at times, to further ideological commitments and concerns. But, as Ernest Nagel has pointed out, the fact "that the interests of the scientist determine what he selects for investigation . . . by itself, represents no obstacle to the successful pursuit of objectively controlled inquiry in any branch of study."[32] Indeed, the assertion that a scientist's values may color his conclusions is intelligible only on the assumption that there exists a distinction between factual and normative statements and that, in principle, it is possible to distinguish between them. It makes no sense to say that all knowlege is subjective unless, in line with the principle of significant contrast, there exists at least the possibility of objective knowledge.

In a suggestive analogy, Karl Popper has compared the status of truth in the objective sense, as correspondence to facts, to that of a mountain peak which is permanently, or almost permanently, wrapped in clouds:

> The climber may not merely have difficulties in getting there — he may not know when he gets there, because he may be unable to distinguish, in the clouds, between the main summit and some subsidiary peak. Yet this does not affect the objective existence of the summit, and if the climber tells us, "I have some doubts whether I reached the actual summit," then he does, by implication, recognize the objective existence of the summit. The very idea of error, or of doubt (in its normal straightforward sense) implies the idea of an objective truth which we may fail to reach.[33]

Similarly, one cannot assert that bourgeois ideology is biased without accepting a distinction between biased and unbiased thinking and thus admitting that such bias, in principle, can be overcome.[34] It is somewhat paradoxical that while Marxists deny the possibility of objective knowledge in the social sciences in general, they claim that Marxism can produce just such scientific truth since it represents *the* science of society.

To be sure, many of the categories used by social scientists are indeed not value-free. When economists or sociologists speak of the "hard-core unemployed," for example, they make the implicit judgment that it would cost too much money to find work for such members of the under-class. Similarly, terms like "democracy" or "revolution" or "genocide" have evaluative connotations. Yet in principle as well as in actual practice, it is possible for the social scientist to employ terminology that is essentially value-free.[35] Or, to put it differently, although complete objectivity and impartiality are probably never fully attainable, the scholar should pursue these goals of scholarship as if they could be realized, and he will be judged by his success in achieving the disinterested pursuit of truth.[36]

The degree to which the scholar has overcome his biases can always be more or less a matter of debate. But the self-corrective mechanisms of science as a social enterprise can go a long way toward minimizing the problem of bias. The scholar is subject to certain canons of correct reasoning and technical competence that will help determine the validity of his results — he must take into account all material relevant to his topic, his findings must be in accord with evidence open to independent check, he should always ask himself what rival interpretation of the evidence might alter his conclusions, and so forth. To the extent that a scholar abides by these rules of his craft he will be considered a good, indifferent, or bad scholar. It is the existence of these rules and the expectation that they will be followed that distinguishes the social sciences, or even the writing of history, from the creative arts.[37] As the former Marxist, Leszek Kolakowski, has pointed out, one should, of course, not expect too much from the observance of such formal, technical requirements of scholarship:

> Such a humble code cannot eliminate disagreement derived from fundamental biases; it can, however, eliminate a good deal of purely ideological or simply dishonest work. To be satisfied with the general assertion that everything in the social and human sciences is purely and simply determined by political preferences and interests — as is common among those who advocate the subordination of the university to political assignments, said to be in any case inevitable — is to deny, against the obvious evidence, the ability of human reason to act according to the rules that it has itself created. This kind of protestant belief in the irreversible corruption of the human mind is, however, self-destructive; it can only avoid the antinomy of the liar if it is supplemented by the belief in another, incorruptible source of knowledge or divine origin, though the advocates of the totalitarian university today rarely seek this kind of assistance.[38]

Lastly, radical academics question the objectivity of the results of scientific inquiry by alleging that the consequences of such work are always political and hence ideological and partial. Here again, we deal with a logical confusion, for the fact that a certain finding of science or a historical account favors the interests of a certain group says nothing about the truth of these conclusions and does not establish that they lack objectivity.[39] The recent findings of some historians, for example, that the Reichstag (the German Parliament building) in 1933 may indeed have been set afire by the Dutch Communist Van der Lubbe and not by the Nazis undoubtedly has been a bonanza to neo-Nazi groups in Germany who have used these accounts to cast doubt on other accusations against the Hitler regime. But whether these findings are true, whether they are objectively demonstrated and established, has absolutely nothing to do with their political significance. Too much of the evidence may have been lost, and we may therefore never be able to reach final certainty on the question of who burned the Reichstag; but in principle we know how to pursue such an inquiry, and its outcome need not and should not be affected by the question whose interests will be advanced by one conclusion rather than another.

Not all arguments against the possibility of objective scientific knowledge are politically inspired, but the attack of some segments of the Left on the objectivity of "bourgeois science" indeed appears primarily to serve to justify and excuse political indoctrination. Instead of proving that higher education promotes the interests of the dominant class and that their disregard of objectivity and impartiality is therefore perfectly in line with ongoing practice in the academy, many radical academics have revealed their contempt for what at one time were uncontested and generally accepted standards of professional conduct and scholarly integrity. This charge does not, of course, apply to all radical or Marxist scholars. Marxist premises can be very fertile for historical inquiry in particular, and in the hands of scholars like Christopher Hill, Eric J. Hobsbawm, Maurice Dobb, Eugene D. Genovese, and others the economic interpretation of history has been a valuable tool of analysis. On the other hand, for less capable minds this same materialist approach to history will often lead to uselessly vague or impossibly precise findings. This means that, in the first case, they will lack any definite implications for historical reality, and, in the second, they will achieve testability at the price of falsity.[40]

Testability and falsifiability as criteria of scientific knowledge and truth are scorned by most Marxists, and for good reason. Their basic concepts have become for them unfalsifiable dogmas; Marxism, while claiming to be a science, has turned into a faith. Hence, like all believers, many Marxists will oppose the test of falsifiability. "If you insist," the philospher Ernest Gellner points out, "that a believer specifies the conditions in which his faith would cease to be true, you implicitly force him to conceive a world in which his faith is *sub judice*, at the mercy of some 'facts' or other. But this is precisely what faiths, total outlooks, systematically avoid and evade."[41]

The commitment of science to rationality and respect for evidence can also be said to be an article of faith. "The means available to our science," acknowledged Max Weber, "offer nothing to those persons to whom this truth is of no value."[42] But a belief in the value of scientific truth is in a class by itself because it is essential for the acquisition of knowledge. There exists a prima facie case for rationality. Without a strong conviction concerning the value of a "due regard for truth" there can be no rational defense of any knowledge whatever.[43] Nonevidential ways of believing may have a place in religion and philosophy, but they are manifestly self-defeating in the sciences. Indeed, on the level of theory, even Marxists will embrace the value of rationality though many of them oppose the use of this same rational method as a test of their own dogmatic beliefs.

Many radical academics today no longer practice a "due regard for truth." Some of them, as the German communist professors discussed in chapter 4 of this study, function essentially as propagandists for the German Democratic Republic and the Soviet Union. Truth for them is that which advances the interests of socialism and communism. Words are used in consciously dishonest ways. Statements like "The Soviet press is the freest in the world," as George Orwell pointed out many years ago, "are

almost always made with intent to deceive."[44] But these communist professors are not the only ones who have abandoned a respect for evidence. A
sociologist who discusses the issues of crime and pollution in America as if
they were a direct result of capitalism disregards data from other social
and political systems that reveal the same social problems and thus engages in distortion rather than scholarly analysis. To praise the communist
regimes of Cuba and Vietnam without mentioning the plight of political
prisoners in these countries amounts to disrespect for evidence. To discuss
leftist theories in terms of their ideological claims and slogans and without
assessing their costs and consequences in terms of human suffering —
something that is invariably and properly done when dealing with rightist
and fascist ideologies — represents a breach of scholarly integrity.[45] When
a Marxist political scientist, Bertell Ollman, writes, "People play no
greater role in their political life than they did in Marx's time. . . . Socially,
class, nation, religion and race remain prisons from which each individual
must escape in order to establish truly human relations," he not only
makes a fairly meaningless political judgment, to which he is entitled, but
he also comes perilously close to the kind of polemical overkill that a true
scholar should disdain.[46]

It is thus useful to distinguish between Marxist scholarship, which can
be valuable, and the use of Marxist categories for purposes of ideological
indoctrination and agitation. In recent years, West German courts several
times have used this distinction in denying diplomas to Marxist students
whose theses had been rejected by their professors for failing to meet minimum standards of scientific integrity. For example, a thesis on "The Influence of the 1966–67 Recession on the Policy of the Trade Unions in the
Federal Republic of Germany" was graded "failed" by Professor Hans-
Joachim Arndt, a political scientist at the University of Heidelberg in
1972. The court, to which the student appealed, upheld the professor's
finding that the thesis exhibited an uncritical acceptance of dogmatic
Marxist positions and was characterized by an agitatory manner. The scientific search for truth, a search which is never ended, said the court in its
opinion, does not necessarily rule out the use of the method of historical
materialism. However, in this case the premises of the inquiry were based
on a political confession and dogmatism; the conclusions were not substantiated by evidence that could stand up under intersubjective scrutiny, and
the work lacked any kind of critical and detached examination of reality.
The secondary literature relied upon was one-sided; the statistics intro-
duced as evidence were used in a misleading manner. In all, this thesis represented an unacceptable "partisan science" (*parteiliche Wissenschaft*)
rather than true scholarship.[47] Similar reasoning was used by a Bremen
court in the case of the Maoist student discussed in chapter 4 of this study.

As I mentioned earlier in this chapter, we do not really know to what extent teachers are able to influence the political thinking of their charges. Most evidence suggests, writes a student of the subject, "that college experiences do not rework youth so that their initial characteristics are totally obliterated; what an individual is when he enters college amounts to most of what he is when he leaves."[48] And yet, it would be surprising if young people were to remain entirely unaffected by a consistent questioning of the values of objectivity and rationality. When such radical scepticism is coupled with a pattern of unmitigated faultfinding concerning the workings of American society, the door is opened to political disillusionment and cynicism, attitudes displayed by many students today. The severe problems this society has faced in the last decade or so — the deterioration of the cities, ghetto riots, the war in Vietnam, and the Watergate scandal — might well have created a crisis of legitimacy in the best of circumstances. But this crisis was blown out of all proportion by those who saw these difficulties not as challenges to be overcome but as proof of our moral depravity. It may well be, writes the political scientist Stanley Rothman,

> that those in the general population who suspect that the deterioration of our social life is related in some degree to the fact that the intellectual community (including academics) has been telling us for some years how rotten we really area, are not entirely in error. The influence of one or another teacher is unimportant, but when the loudest voices in the intellectual community are committed to exposing the falsity of the values which sustain us, and documenting every wart on the body politic, it is not unreasonable to suspect that they may be helping to create the malaise they claim to be documenting.[49]

The number of radical academics in American colleges and universities remains relatively small, but, together with some of those who call themselves liberal and who often hold very similar negative attitudes toward the traditional values of American society, they do amount to a strong influence, especially in elite schools. In whatever way one may wish to assess the long-range consequences of all this, one thing is rather clear: American higher education today is not a stronghold of capitalist domination and its impact means anything but a strengthening of the status quo. The great expansion of the college population has created millions of new "intellectuals," many of whom hold an adversary posture toward the society in which they live. Indeed, since the end of the 1960s it has ceased to be clear which attitudes represent conformity or nonconformity: the traditional support for existing social institutions and values or their reflexive disparagement.[50] The cultural hegemony of the capitalist class, if it ever existed, no longer exists today. The American system of education not only does not produce "false consciousness," but it encourages the kind of self-doubt that, left unchecked, will undermine democratic values and institutions.

Notes

1. Benjamin Floyd Pittenger, *Indoctrination for American Democracy* (New York, 1941), p. 1.
2. Michael Parenti, *Power and the Powerless* (New York, 1978), p. 47.
3. Sidney Hook, *Education for Modern Man: A New Perspective*, rev. ed. (New York, 1963), p. ix.
4. Ibid., p. 89.
5. Samuel Bowles and Herbert Gintis, *Schooling in Capitalist America: Educational Reform and the Contradictions of Economic Life* (New York, 1976), p. 11.
6. Neil Postman, "The Politics of Reading," in Nell Keddie, ed., *Tinker, Tailor ... The Myth of Cultural Deprivation* (Hammondsworth, 1973), p. 88.
7. Cf. Christopher J. Hurn, *Limits and Possibilities of Schooling: An Introduction to the Sociology of Education* (Boston, 1978), p. 202.
8. Ibid., p. 189.
9. Kenneth P. Langton and M. Kent Jennings, "Political Socialization and the High School Civics Curriculum in the United States," *American Political Science Review*, LXII (1968): 852–67.
10. Dean Jaros, *Socialization to Politics* (New York, 1973), p. 98. See also Byron G. Massialas, *Education and the Political System* (Reading, Mass., 1969), who criticizes the different conclusions of Robert D. Hess and Judith V. Torney, *The Development of Political Attitudes in Children* (Chicago, 1967).
11. Hurn, op. cit., p. 78.
12. Cf. Fred H. Hechinger, "Wave of Censors Hits the Schools," *New York Times*, May 8, 1979. According to Edward B. Jenkinson, *Censors in the Classroom: The Mind Benders* (Carbondale, Ill., 1979), at least 200 organizations now work at the local, state, and national level to remove textbooks and courses that they consider offensive.
13. Richard E. Gross, "The Status of the Social Studies in the Public Schools of the United States: Facts and Impressions of a National Survey," *Social Education*, XLI (1977): 199.
14. Karen Smith Dawson, "Political Education — A Challenge," *News for Teachers of Political Science*, no. 20 (Winter 1978), p. 4.
15. Frances FitzGerald, *America Revised: History Schoolbooks in the Twentieth Century* (Boston, 1979), p. 11.
16. Martin F. Herz, *How the Cold War is Taught: Six American History Textbooks Examined* (Washington, D.C., 1978), p. 72.
17. Bowles and Gintis, op. cit., p. 12.
18. Harold Entwistle, *Class, Culture and Education* (London, 1978), p. 97.
19. Peter Blau and Otis Dudley Duncan, *The American Occupational Structure* (New York, 1967).
20. Christopher Jencks et al., *Who Gets Ahead? The Determinants of Economic Success in America* (New York, 1979).
21. Henry Phelps Brown, *The Inequality of Pay* (Berkeley, Calif., 1977), pp. 253–54.
22. This is the argument pressed by Richard H. deLone, *Small Futures: Children, Inequality, and the Limits of Liberal Reform* (New York, 1979). The quote is from a review of this book by Diane Ravich in the *New York Times Book Review*, September 16, 1979. See also Ravich's book, *The Revisionists Revised: A Critique of the Radical Attack on the Schools* (New York, 1978).

23. Basil B. Bernstein, "Social Class, Language and Socialisation," in Thomas A. Sebeok, ed., *Current Trends in Linguistics*, vol. XII, part 3 (The Hague, 1974), p. 1550.
24. Entwistle, op. cit., p. 190.
25. Cf. M. Kent Jennings and Richard G. Niemi, *The Political Character of Adolescence: The Influence of Families and Schools* (Princeton, N.J., 1974), p. 331.
26. Everett C. Ladd, Jr. and Seymour M. Lipset, *The Divided Academy: Professors and Politics* (New York, 1975), Table 2, p. 26.
27. From a flyer advertising Howard Zinn, *Postwar America: 1945–1971* (Indianapolis, 1973).
28. Theodor Mills Norton and Bertell Ollman, eds., *Studies in Socialist Pedagogy* (New York, 1978), pp. 276, 278.
29. Ibid., p. 248.
30. James Scofield and Michael Yates, "Teaching Marxists to Teach," *Monthly Review*, vol. XXX, no. 9 (February, 1979), pp. 60–61.
31. Cf. Heinz Eulau, "The Politicization of Everything: On the Limits of Politics in Political Education," in Vernon van Dyke, ed., *Teaching Political Science: The Professor and the Polity* (Atlantic Highlands, N.J., 1977), p. 59.
32. Ernest Nagel, *The Structure of Science: Problems in the Logic of Scientific Explanation* (New York, 1961), pp. 486–87.
33. Karl Popper, *Conjectures and Refutations: The Growth of Scientific Knowledge* (New York, 1968), p. 226.
34. Cf. R. F. Atkinson, *Knowledge and Explanation in History: An Introduction to the Philosophy of History* (Ithaca, N.Y., 1978), p. 79; W. G. Runciman, *A Critique of Max Weber's Philosophy of Social Science* (Cambridge, 1972), p. 58.
35. For some examples see Felix E. Oppenheim, " 'Facts' and 'Values' in Politics: Are They Separable?" *Political Theory* I (1973): 55–59.
36. Cf. Alan Montefiore, ed., *Neutrality and Impartiality: The University and Political Commitment* (London, 1975), p. 27.
37. Gordon Leff, *History and Social Theory* (Garden City, N.Y., 1971), pp. 109–10.
38. Leszek Kolakowski, "Neutrality and Academic Values," in Montefiore, op. cit., p. 82.
39. Cf. Göran Hermerén, "Criteria of Objectivity in History," *Danish Yearbook of Philosophy*, XIV (1977): 28.
40. Atkinson, op. cit., p. 81.
41. Ernest Gellner, *Legitimation of Belief* (London, 1974), p. 176.
42. Max Weber, " 'Objectivity' in Social Science and Social Policy," in Maurice Natanson, ed., *Philosophy of the Social Sciences: A Reader* (New York, 1963), p. 417.
43. Cf. Thomas F. Green, "Indoctrination and Belief," in I. A. Snook, ed., *Concepts of Indoctrination: Philosophical Essays* (London, 1972), p. 42.
44. George Orwell, "Politics and the English Language," *A Collection of Essays* (Garden City, N.Y., 1954), p. 169.
45. This example is given by Henry Novotny in a contribution to Sidney Hook et al., eds., *The Ethics of Teaching and Scientific Research* (Buffalo, N.Y., 1977), p. 68.
46. The quote is from Bertell Ollman, *Alienation: Marx's Conception of Man in Capitalist Society* (Cambridge, 1971), p. 245. My attention to it was drawn

by Thomas H. Magstadt, "Can a Marxist be a Political Science Chairman?" *Chronicle of Higher Education* (February 20, 1979), p. 21.

47. Verwaltungsgerichtshof Baden-Württemberg, Opinion of July 1, 1975 — IV 951/73.
48. Jaros, op. cit., p. 128.
49. Stanley Rothman, "Mainstream Political Science and its Discontents," in Van Dyke, op. cit, p. 28.
50. Cf. Paul Hollander, *Political Pilgrims: Travels of Western Intellectuals to the Soviet Union, China and Cuba 1928–1978* (New York, 1981), p. 24.

CHAPTER 7

The Mass Media in America

In addition to the American system of education, the mass media in America — press, radio and television — have also been blamed for creating a false sense of reality and misleading people into supporting the political and economic status quo. In the eyes of many radicals, the managers of the media produce manipulated messages that secure popular support "for a social order that is not in the majority's long-term interest."[1] Conservatives, on the other hand, argue that the media have become part of a new adversary culture, hostile to business and sanctioning the values of the counterculture, and they call attention to what they regard as the liberal bias of the media.[2]

The Concept of Bias

The efforts of journalists to make their reporting objective and balanced — part of their professional code of conduct — may explain why the media are so frequently attacked from both the Left and the Right; these efforts to be fair generally lead to stories that do not reflect the views of any one interest group.[3] Moreover, while lying and willful omissions and distortions are clear violations of the norms of objectivity and impartiality, it is by no means easy to ascertain the presence of less obvious bias or even to agree on a definition of bias in reporting.

It is useful here to distinguish between political and structural bias. The latter arises, first of all, from the fact that all communication is necessarily selective. Radio and television can never report "all the facts," nor can newspapers convey "all the news that's fit to print." Selectivity involves assumptions held by reporters, editors, and producers about what is important and newsworthy, and such assumptions will necessarily be shaped by these individuals' ingrained beliefs and views of the world. "In this sense, 'purely objective' reporting is impossible."[4] Second, structural bias involves constraints inherent in the medium itself. Radio and television producers, for example, must live within a budget that is always restrictive; reporters must operate in a framework of limited time for the writing of stories or for news broadcasting; programs must attract a sponsor and a large number of viewers to bring in the advertising revenue on which the media depend, and these commercial considerations put a premium on drama, action, and other elements that make for massive audiences.[5]

Many of the complaints registered against the media are thus related to structural and organizational imperatives imposed by the nature of the medium. Yet there also is such a thing as political bias. All reporting is selective, and the summary account of, say, a political speech by a candidate for high political office will never be as objective as the published text of the complete speech, derived from a recording by a mechanical device that has no political preferences. Yet some accounts will be more objective than others. Unjustifiable omissions of important points in the speech or deliberate exaggeration of other parts for the purpose of damaging the reputation of the candidate will be evidence of the existence of political bias. It may be difficult, Sidney Hook has pointed out, to define in a positive way what constitutes "fairness" in the exposition of a controversial theme:

> But it is not difficult to detect elements of unfairness in what purports to be a balanced presentation. For example, if one side is given more time than the other, or if one side is allowed opportunity to rebut the other but not vice versa, or if protagonists of different positions are selected in such a way that one is more articulate or audible or well spoken than the other — when it is easily possible to match them in these respects — it is obvious that the claim to fairness is a pretence and a sham.[6]

In many concrete cases the determination of bias will be difficult. Certainly unfavorable coverage of a subject does not by itself establish political bias. One would not expect that murderers, liars, corrupt officials, inefficient generals, and the like would be depicted as examples of high morality or worthy achievement. Content analysis that counts the number of favorable and unfavorable references to a certain item and ignores the appropriateness of the content as compared to reality by itself can therefore never resolve the question of bias.[7] Yet despite these difficulties, the ideals of fairness, impartiality, and balance are there to be pursued, and the charge of political bias and prejudice can frequently be proven. The findings of the National News Council, established in 1973 to assess complaints of bias against the media, very often leave no doubt that a violation of professional norms has occurred.

Content analysis can suggest possible bias, but even a finding that a certain news item or program was characterized by political bias does not prove that the item or program was successful in passing on the bias. Content analysis can suggest possible effects, but it cannot be a substitute for audience research aimed at establishing actual effects. "Documentation that news programming plays up crime or contains liberal bias is never proof that television news causes violence or produces left-leaning voters."[8]

The Impact of the Media on the Electoral Process

With regard to elections, the much-vaunted "power of the media" is largely a myth. Throughout American history it has not been unusual for presidents to be elected while a majority of the country's newspapers were lined up in opposition to them. Franklin D. Roosevelt, for example, was never supported by more than 26 percent of the total newspaper circulation. In the 1960 election, 731 of the daily newspapers with 71 percent of the circulation editorially supported Richard Nixon, and only 208 dailies with 16 percent of the circulation favored John F. Kennedy. If newspaper support was truly crucial, Nixon should have been the overwhelming winner in what in fact turned out to be a very close contest won by Kennedy.[9] While television has helped some men into office, it has not been nearly as important as the accidental factors that usually are decisive and that television can merely make a little more useful. For example, Senator Charles Percy of Illinois has been blessed with good looks, verbal dexterity, and wealth, but television could not turn these qualities into conditions of success; in 1968 Percy remained the least favored of the contenders for the Republican presidential nomination. Other accidents, such as that of birth, also remain unaffected by technological innovations such as the advent of television. It is still useful to be called Long in Louisiana, Byrd in Virginia or LaFollette in Wisconsin. Media exposure does not change the force of these chance factors, and neither can it overcome the handicap of espousing a position that is no longer favored by the electorate.[10] Senator Edward Kennedy with his advocacy of more government spending found himself running up against the tide of such a general sentiment in 1980.

A study of the role of television in the 1972 presidential election has demonstrated the limited importance of this medium. Neither the network evening news nor political commercials had much of an impact on the electorate, and this was true for both committed as well as initially undecided voters. Despite the great number of spot ads used in the campaign, only about 3 percent of the electorate was influenced at all by political advertising, and even these few were not necessarily manipulated. For voters least interested in and least informed about politics, these ads contributed substantial amounts of factual information and increased their awareness of the issues.[11]

The media not only do not decide elections, but they are also largely unsuccessful in changing or affecting strongly held attitudes. During the period 1948–56, V. O. Key found, the media were strongly opposed to "socialized medicine," but a substantial majority of the population was in favor of some type of government action in the health field. In fact, those persons most exposed to the media were also the least affected by the latter's editorial stands. The same finding held true for attitudes toward the government's responsibility for assuring employment.[12] A more recent example of the same phenomenon is the popular reaction to the behavior of the police during the street demonstrations in Chicago at the time of the 1968 Democratic convention. Despite the fact that most of the media were outspokenly critical of the conduct of the police, the public widely applauded what some of the media had called a "police riot."[13] Clearly, reality casts strong doubt on the Orwellian image of a population dominated, managed, and brainwashed by the media, whether it be in the interests of the capitalists or of anyone else.

There are several reasons why mass communication is more likely to reinforce existing opinions than to change them. Research has shown that, by and large, people pay attention to those messages with which they agree. Material not in accord with their existing attitudes and values is either ignored or quickly forgotten or reinterpreted to fit existing views. These are the screens of selective exposure, selective retention, and selective perception, of which the latter is probably the best known. A good description of selective perception at work is provided by a student of television:

> Any person who has been in a room filled with die-hard Republicans and Democrats, watching television while a President justifies his actions on a controversial partisan policy, knows firsthand the impact of selective perception. One group sees sincerity and concern in every gesture, expression, and inflection. The other sees manipulation, crass politics, insincerity. They are watching the same President make the same movements and say the same things, but they might as well be viewing a different person.[14]

The messages of the media, many studies have demonstrated, do not strike an atomized, helpless mass of individuals at the mercy of an all-powerful institution but, if they reach their target at all, do speak to persons involved in a network of personal relationships, which strongly affect their outlook on the world, including the messages of the media. The values we share with family, friends, and various groups to which we belong intervene between the communications of the media and our reaction to them. Group norms and personal influence of this kind, it turns out, have a stronger hold on us and are far more effective in molding our thinking than the media because they come from sources that are more in tune with our personal likes and dislikes, from persons whom we trust because they are close to us.[15]

As I have mentioned earlier, persons most attentive to the media are also the least affected by them. Such individuals are likely to compare information received from the mass media with that from other sources, and they will therefore be critical and less receptive to persuasion. On the other hand, persons with little education and lower intelligence — "mass man"

— whom radical writers have pictured as most defenseless and susceptible to manipulation by the media, turn out to be less influenced for the simple reason that they pay less attention to the media. Not surprisingly, children are more persuadable than adults, but research on the links between persuadability and characteristics such as religion, race, and social class has found no significant correlations.[16] Here again, the image of the media as instruments of evil design and as a powerful force lulling millions of poor people into a complacent acceptance of capitalist ideology is not substantiated by the evidence.

The Media and the Ethos of Society

And yet, it would be a mistake to conclude that because the mass media are not all-powerful they are without any impact at all on the socialization process and on public opinion. First, while the mass media may not be successful in telling us what to think, they appear to do rather well in telling us what to think about. In 1972, according to the Roper poll, 64 percent of the general public derived most of their news about the world from television.[17] This has created a situation in which the media, especially television, have an important role in deciding what is newsworthy. What the producers and editors of television news decide to mention and to show on television screens tends to become "the news" and "the" subject of interest. The media have come "to define the terms, issues, and especially the priorities of public discussion"[18] — they set the agenda of public debate.

Second, politics involves more than elections. Although the media do not determine the outcome of electoral contests, television in particular appears to have a subtle impact on the general ethos of the society in which we live. In part this is the result of what earlier we called a structural bias of television — which leads to bad news, with its crises and dangers, taking precedence over good news. All of the media underreport progress, but this is especially the case with television, which will achieve a larger audience through the presentation of menacing events and the cultivation of suspense and drama than with happy tidings.[19] The saying "good news is no news" thus has considerable validity.

In recent times the tendency of journalists to see themselves not only as defenders of the people but also as champions of good causes has reinforced the structural bias inherent in the medium. The populist heritage of America has always meant that reporters who won prizes were those who exposed graft and corruption. New and different is the emphasis of many journalists upon drawing attention to what is wrong with our society, upon taking on not only corrupt public officials but the entire social order.

Several years ago, in a speech to a university audience, the television newscaster Roger Mudd defined the mission of journalism in these terms:

> What the national media, and mainly television, have done is to believe that their chief duty is to put before the nation its unfinished business: pollution, the Vietnam War, discrimination, continuing violence, motor traffic, slums. The media have become the nation's critics, and as critics no political administration, regardless of how hard it tries, will satisfy them.[20]

As insatiable critics such reporters not only expose specific wrongdoing, but they become part of the adversary culture, which is never content with whatever government does. These journalists become the people's self-appointed tribunes, engaged in a perpetual confrontation with the country's institutions and public authority.

How many reporters have embraced this new calling cannot be determined, but we do know that journalists today, like college professors, are well to the left of the population at large. A survey taken in 1971 of print and electronic journalists found that of those working for the prominent news services, newspapers, magazines and the three television networks, 63 percent of the executives and 53 percent of the staffers defined themselves as left of center, while only 10 percent of the executives and 17 percent of the staffers viewed themselves as right of center.[21] Similar findings come from a survey of foreign correspondents made in 1967.[22]

The degree to which the journalists' political preferences influence their reporting is difficult to judge. It may well be that the media's extensive and often favorable coverage of the civil rights movement, the women's movement, the environmental movement, antiwar agitation, and the counterculture simply reflects the consequences of the profit motive, because radical and offbeat ideas and obtrusive activities such as demonstrations create dramatic news sure to expand audiences and circulations. Not surprisingly, a study of the Minneapolis media during the first 10 months of 1970 found that minority groups such as blacks and Students for a Democratic Society received more publicity than comparable establishment groups like the American Legion or the League of Women voters.[23] "The system's long-term interests," the sociologist Alvin W. Gouldner has argued, "are sold out for short-term profits."[24] Intended or not, the fact remains that the media have helped publicize new ways of thinking and acting, and they have probably played a part, however difficult to measure, in making this new culture more acceptable.

Another case in point is the consumer movement in America, which was given a tremendous boost by extensive publicity about the efforts of General Motors to silence the consumer advocate Ralph Nader. Despite Nader's avowed hostility to business and in the face of the much-vaunted power of business advertisers, Nader achieved headlines and has remained in the news ever since. Whether one explains this phenomenon in terms of the media's hunger for the novel and unusual or whether one assumes that reporters liked Nader because they saw him as the "enemy of their enemies,"[25] it is a fact that for many years now the consumer movement has received generous publicity. The advances and achievements of consumerism probably would have been unthinkable without this help provided by the media. The extensive publicity given to the counterculture as well as to dissenting political and social movements certainly undercuts Herbert Marcuse's central argument of a totalitarian and "one-dimensional" manipulation of public opinion.

Some students of the media see a connection between this openness to new ideas and attitudes and the liberal media people who are in positions of creative authority. Television writers and producers, a man who has lived with them for some time has observed, consider themselves at odds with an establishment made up of the exploitative rich and the multinational corporations. As a result, crimes on television generally are committed by well-to-do men in three-piece suits; the military, especially officers, are pictured as bumbling bureaucrats at best; the poor are depicted as saintly and trustworthy, and few acts of wrongdoing are carried out by blacks or chicanos. "The same kind of reasoning which lifts from criminals the burden for criminal behavior relieves poor people of the onus of their poverty. All blame is placed on society, because of either society's plotting or society's neglect."[26]

A similar view is taken by the political scientist Stanley Rothman, who sees pivotal members of the media elite sharing what he calls a liberal-cosmopolitan paradigm. The paradigm tells them what the world should be like and leads them to see and judge events in certain predictable ways. The paradigm of such journalists includes a distrust of business, of technology, of the military, and of anyone who is overly patriotic, as well as a benevolent view of those in favor of social change, no matter how radical their tactics. As Walter Cronkite put it in an interview: "As far as the leftist thing is concerned, that I think is something that comes from the nature of a journalist's work. . . . I think that they are inclined to side with humanity rather than with authority and institutions."[27]

There is some evidence, Rothman suggests, that the general outlines of this paradigm have begun to take on the quality of reality for viewers of television, and the fact that this same paradigm is shared by many who taught them in college increases the influence of what they read in newspapers and see on television. The effects are potentially serious. "Middle-class youth are now by and large convinced that America is a seriously flawed society, and their reaction has been a shift to the left or, more recently, a withdrawal from political activity into personal concerns."[28] Much the same conclusion was reached by another political scientist, Michael D. Robinson, in an empirical study published in 1976, which sees a link between the public's increased reliance on television, on one hand, and the decline in political trust and the spread of gloom and pessimism about the future of our society on the other. Basing his conclusions on laboratory investigations and survey data, Robinson found that television journalism increasingly causes "frustration, cynicism, self-doubt, and malaise." The network news departments, on account of economic and organizational imperatives (structural bias) and, to a lesser extent, reflecting the personal and partisan objectives of their staff, produce a content that is "dramatic, negativistic, contentious, and disestablishmentarian." Robinson doubts that the data of Edith Efron's controversial study, *The News Twisters*, confirm her charge of television favoritism for the "Democratic-Liberal-Left axis of opinion," but he sees these data revealing a bias that is anti-institutional and disestablishmentarian. These "anti-institutional themes reach the audience with one essential message: none of our national policies work, none of our institutions respond, none of our political organizations succeed."[29]

The media's role as a critic of society has been reinforced in recent years by the emergence of a new alternative or "underground" media sector. As a result of the development of the photo-offset process, which involves the "photographing" of typed pages, it is now possible to produce a newspaper at a very nominal cost. In 1970 the number of such alternative newspapers was estimated at more than 450, and they reached a combined circulation of five million readers. Some of these papers rely on local advertising and are distributed free; others are sold at a modest price. Many of them are produced by young people, sympathetic to a radical and countercultural outlook. The "underground" press, a student of the subject has written, "has shown that the economic requirements for publishing a newspaper need not be a matter of real concern for those intent on communicating their point of view."[30] This observation is strengthened by the existence of a strong socialist and communist press in those capitalist countries where these parties of the Left have a large popular following. In other words, the failure of Marxist ideas to take root in America cannot be blamed on the alleged monopoly of capitalists in the ownership of the media.

The Case of the Vietnam War

The trauma of the Vietnam war undoubtedly has weakened faith in America's political and social institutions, but here, too, the media may have increased the malaise. During the first few years of the American involvement, both the press and television were largely supportive of the war. Television documentaries like the CBS program "Vietnam Perspective: Air War in the North," screened in February 1967, provided strong support for the role and style of American air power in Vietnam.[31] Reports unfavorable to the American side, such as Morley Safer's famous coverage of U.S. Marines setting fire to a Vietnamese hamlet in August 1965 or Harrison Salisbury's reporting for the *New York Times* on the bombing of North Vietnam in December 1966, were uncommon. Years later David Halberstam called the televised hearings on U.S. Vietnam policy before the Senate Foreign Relations Committee in February 1966 "a rare alliance of the media and another political institution [Congress] against the presidency," and he observed that the hearings helped legitimate dissent on the war.[32] Indeed, as the social critic Robert Paul Wolff pointed out at the time, even during this early period, when both the media and the public were still predominantly backing official policy, the assumption, popular with radicals, of an electorate manipulated into passivity and acquiescence by way of an elaborate apparatus of indoctrination was "totally unsupported by the facts."

> The official government justification of our Vietnamese policy has been regularly and explicitly refuted by news reports for almost two years now. The dictatorial character of the South Vietnamese military junta is displayed nightly in televised news broadcasts which reach tens of millions of American homes. Vivid images of the torturing of captives, the suppression of Buddhist groups, the burning of villages, are forced upon the American consciousness. News commentators repeatedly remind their audiences of the chasm between the predictions of our military advisers and the actual course of events. The hostile questioning of Administration witnesses by dissenting senators preempts revenue-producing afternoon and evening programs, so that Americans are virtually forced to acquaint themselves with the anti-government views of highly respected political figures. Those citizens whose political interest prompts them to even the slightest effort need only pick up the *New York Times* to read condemnations of the war as vigorous as any published in left-wing journals of protest. The bookstands are crowded with more dissenting literature on the subject than anyone could want to read.[33]

The media began to express increasing doubts on the trend of events in the summer of 1967, and the real turning point came during the Tet offensive early in 1968. From a strictly military point of view, the communist offensive was a defeat for the Viet Cong. The general uprising on which they had counted failed to materialize, and only in the case of Hue were they able to hold on to an objective for any appreciable length of time. By the end of February enemy losses had reached 37,000 killed. But the coverage of this offensive by television helped turn this defeat into a debacle for the American and South Vietnamese side. The nightly pictures of ruined and smoking cities, of house-to-house fighting, of violence and gore and the seemingly imminent annihilation of the besieged marines at Khe Sanh combined to convey a sense of defeat and impending disaster. Even when it had become clear to reporters in the field that the South Vietnamese had in fact not been routed, the general line of media coverage in the United States remained one of collapse and doom.[34] "The oracles of American society, the commentators, editorial writers and leaders of private America, many of whom had been uneasy and uncertain before," wrote Don Ober-dorfer, who had observed the amazing performance of the media on the spot, "now became convinced that the war was being lost or, at the very best, could not be won."[35] Walter Cronkite, the pundit of American news-casters, returned from a visit to Vietnam persuaded that all was beyond hope. "It was the first time in American history that a war had been de-clared over by a commentator."[36] The loss of Cronkite is said to have solidi-fied President Johnson's decision not to seek reelection.

In late 1968, Jack Fern, a field producer for NBC, proposed to head-quarters a series showing that Tet had in fact been a military victory for the Americans and that the media had mistakenly created the impression of an allied defeat. Robert J. Northshield, the producer of NBC News, re-jected the idea because, as he said later, Tet was by then "established in the public's mind as a defeat, and therefore it was an American defeat."[37] In a sense, Northshield was right. The media, in a rare demonstration of great power, had indeed succeeded in convincing opinion leaders and large segments of the general public that the Tet offensive had resulted in an al-lied rout. Gallup Poll data suggest that between early February and the middle of March 1968 nearly one person in five switched from the "hawk" to the "dove" position.[38]

From 1968 until the American withdrawal from Vietnam in 1972, me-dia coverage of the war was not only increasingly pessimistic but also gen-erally very critical of the American war effort. The corrupt Thieu government, not the Hanoi regime, was described as the main villain. The Viet Cong were notoriously uncooperative in allowing Western cameramen to shoot pictures of the disemboweling of village chiefs and other acts of terror, while scenes of South Vietnamese brutality, such as the mistreat-ment of prisoners, were often seen on American television screens. The ten-dency on the part of many newspaper and television reporters to see the war in Vietnam as an atrocity writ large led them to accept and publicize charges of American war crimes even when the evidence was weak or fab-ricated.[39] Americans, essentially unable to check the claims of the Com-munist camp, were left with the image of a tough and highly effective enemy while at the same time they were regularly exposed to the human and bureaucratic errors and shortcomings of their own side. War has al-ways been beastly, but the Vietnam war was the first war exposed to televi-sion cameras and seen practically in every home, often in living color. Not surprisingly, the close-up view of devastation and suffering, repeated al-most daily, strengthened the growing desire for peace.

Some of the studies indicating an antiwar bias on the part of television, in particular, have been criticized on methodological grounds.[40] But even if one puts aside these challenged findings, there remains abundant evidence of bias — both structural and political.[41] Was the American public affected by this bias? In the case of the Tet offensive, as we have seen, the impact of misreporting was powerful and decisive. The results of unfavorable coverage during the following years are more difficult to document, though we have some empirical evidence. A study of the attitudes of high school students toward war in general and the Vietnam war in particular showed that in learning about these subjects they had relied on the mass media twice as often as on any other source. Television was cited as the major media source by half the students.[42] The argument of some conservatives that the war in Vietnam was lost in the American press and on American television screens is undoubtedly giving far too much credit to the media, but that media coverage of the Vietnam war had an impact on public opinion can hardly be doubted. The mass media, writes a political scientist, "did not lead the trend toward dissent, but anyone who believes that it did not report it, exaggerate it and, perhaps unwittingly, foster it must have been living in another country."[43]

Television executives and producers themselves, citing public opinion polls which show that television is now the main as well as the most believed source of news, have taken credit for changing American opinion on the war. One of the more tentative judgments comes from William Small, director of CBS News in Washington: "When Television covered its 'first war' in Vietnam, it showed a terrible truth of war in a manner new to mass audiences. A case can be made, and certainly should be examined, that this was cardinal to the disillusionment of Americans with this war, the cynicism of many young people toward America, and the destruction of Lyndon Johnson's term of office."[44] Somewhat stronger is the conclusion of James Reston who wrote in the *New York Times* on the day of the fall of Saigon: "Maybe the historians will agree that the reporters and the cameras were decisive in the end. They brought the issue of the war to the people, before the Congress and the courts, and forced the withdrawal of American power from Vietnam."[45] Whether this achievement of the media in making history is to be celebrated or regretted depends on one's assessment of the long-range consequences of the American defeat in Vietnam, and the last word on this historic event is not yet in. It can be stated that the effect of the media was gained primarily through the exploitation of emotional feelings rather than by way of encouraging deliberate and rational intellectual judgment on a highly complex issue of public policy. The media triumphed over the political establishment, and this experience once again refutes the radical view of the media as pillars of the ruling class.

Conclusions

The American media today are no longer, if they ever were, simply the mouthpiece of capitalist propaganda. It can no longer be assumed, as did

V. O. Key some 20 years ago, that the major influence of the media upon political attitudes is to reinforce the status quo. Indeed, if the media seek to accomplish this objective, they surely are not doing a very good job; our society today has more rapid social change than at any other time in history. As we have seen, there is good reason to think that the media have an important part in popularizing new attitudes and behaviors and that this leads gradually to revised values and institutional change. The benefits and liabilities of such change can be the subject of debate, but its occurrence can hardly be denied. The actual role of the media in public affairs, including the Dreyfus affair and Watergate, concludes Alvin Gouldner, "is profoundly at variance with any simple-minded stereotype of media simply as an agency reproducing the existing system of domination."[46] The thesis of the power of the media, writes a German radical writer, serves to excuse the failure of the Left[47] and that may explain its popularity with radicals.

As far as the entertainment programs of radio and television are concerned, power in many ways lies with the audience rather than with the producers. The American public is constantly being polled about its views of the entertainment offered, and audience reaction is a crucial determinant of which programs will survive. In the same way, newspapers and magazines learn of consumer desires from their circulation figures.[48] Much of this entertainment may represent escapist fare, but the radical notion that this amusement enslaves the consciousness of the masses[49] is unsupported by any evidence. Indeed, as we have seen above, some of it is openly critical of the rich and powerful and romanticizes the poor and criminal elements. These programs, it appears, do not actually create passivity and apathy among the nonapathetic but merely reinforce the apathy of those already apathetic. "The weight of available evidence seems to favor the view that escapist fare is not the prime cause of any particular way of life, but rather that it serves the psychological needs and reinforces the ways of life already characteristic of its audience."[50]

Could it be that the media manipulate us in so pervasive and subtle a way that it eludes the social scientists as well as everybody else in society? This is, of course, the core meaning of manipulation — control of citizens' views and attitudes by persons whose interests are served by this skillful management of opinions without the awareness of those who are being manipulated, and whose "real" interests are subverted by this control.[51] But no matter how subtly the manipulation is assumed to operate, one would expect that some evidence of its existence could be produced. Otherwise the correctness of this charge would have to be accepted as an article of faith. The fact that the media by and large share society's consensus on ultimate values surely is not proof of manipulation or indoctrination. The burden of proof is upon those who allege manipulation, not upon those who share this consensus.

Moreover, the doctrine of an all-pervasive manipulation runs into the same difficulties noted earlier in our discussion of ideological distortion and emancipatory social science. It is of course *logically* possible for a few enlightened souls to escape manipulation and to qualify as the best judges of the "true interests" of those still suffering from a manipulated perspective. But such a state of affairs not only amounts to what Alasdair MacIntyre has called "epistemological self-righteousness" (see p. 40), but it also has profoundly undemocratic and elitist implications and consequences. Under this view, the manipulated mass of the people clearly cannot be expected to understand and freely accept the criteria with the help of which they could identify those invididuals who are not manipulated. Caught in the ways of thinking of the manipulated society, the masses would not be able to recognize and approve of their emancipators, and the latter would necessarily have to be self-appointed dictators.

Lastly, any claim of the few to be free from manipulation in the realm of values assumes the existence of a standard of moral truth that is opposed to the false consciousness afflicting the many. Leaving aside the manifest philosophical difficulties of this assumption, the way in which throughout history most self-chosen guardians of human morality have implemented their moral vision marks this way out of manipulation as a superbly unattractive option. To reject the argument that people in a democratic society are being subjected to systematic manipulation by the media does not obligate one to deny the existence of bias and other malfeasance on the part of the media. However, the democrat will seek remedies for these shortcomings that do not substitute for an imperfect institution, from the clutches of which one can escape, the equally imperfect rule of philosopher-kings or other dictators unaccountable to popular will.

Notes

1. Herbert I. Schiller, *The Mind Managers* (Boston, 1973), p. 1; see also Robert Cirino, *Don't Blame the People* (Los Angeles, Calif., 1971).
2. Daniel Bell, *The Cultural Contradictions of Capitalism* (New York, 1976), pp. 40–41; George F. Will, ed., *Press, Politics and Popular Government* (Washington, D.C., 1972), p. 8.
3. W. Phillips Davison et al., *Mass Media: Systems and Effects* (New York, 1976), p. 96.
4. C. Richard Hofstetter, *Bias in the News: Network Television Coverage of the 1972 Election Campaign* (Columbus, Ohio, 1976), p. 187.
5. Cf. Edward Jay Epstein, *News From Nowhere: Television and the News* (New York, 1973).
6. Sidney Hook, "The Bias in Public Media Programs," *Measure*, no. 44 (October 1977), p. 3.
7. William C. Adams, "Network News Research in Perspective: A Bibliographical Essay," in William C. Adams and Fay Schreibman, eds., *Television Network News: Issues in Content Research* (Washington, D.C., 1978), p. 20.

8. Thomas E. Patterson, "Assessing Television Newscasts: Future Directions in Content Analysis," in Adams and Schreibman, op. cit., p. 178.
9. Cf. Ben H. Bagdikian, *The Effete Conspiracy and Other Crimes by the Press* (New York, 1972), p. 96.
10. John Whale, *The Half-Shut Eye: Television and Politics in Britain and America* (London, 1969), p. 200.
11. Thomas E. Patterson and Robert D. McClure, *The Unseeing Eye: The Myth of Television Power in National Politics* (New York, 1976), pp. 104–16.
12. V. O. Key, Jr., *Public Opinion and American Democracy* (New York, 1961), pp. 397, 402.
13. Bernard Roshco, *Newsmaking* (Chicago, Ill., 1975), p. 124.
14. Patterson and McClure, op. cit., p. 65; see also Joseph T. Klapper, *The Effects of Mass Communication* (New York, 1960), pp. 18–19.
15. Key, op. cit., pp. 366–67; Elihu Katz and Paul F. Lazarsfeld, *Personal Influence* (Glencoe, Ill., 1955), p. 131.
16. Davison, op. cit., p. 175.
17. The Roper Organization, *What People Think of Television and Other Mass Media: 1959–1972* (New York, 1973), p. 2.
18. Paul H. Weaver, "Is Television Biased?" *The Public Interest*, no. 26 (Winter 1972): 58.
19. Roshco, op. cit., pp. 16–17.
20. Cited by Irving Kristol in Will, op. cit., p. 50.
21. John W. Johnstone et al., *The News People: A Sociological Portrait of American Journalists and their Work* (Urbana, Ill., 1976), p. 93.
22. Leo Bogart, "Survey of Foreign Correspondents," *Journalism Review*, Summer 1968, discussed by Davison, op. cit., p. 89.
23. Fred Fedler, "The Media and Minority Groups: A Study of Adequacy of Access," *Journalism Quarterly*, L (1973): 109–17.
24. Alvin W. Gouldner, *The Dialectics of Ideology and Technology: The Origins, Grammar and Future of Ideology* (New York, 1976), p. 157.
25. Stanley Rothman, "The Mass Media in Post-Industrial Society," in Seymour Martin Lipset, ed., *The Third Century: America as Post-Industrial Society* (Stanford, Calif., 1979), p. 375.
26. Ben Stein, *The View from Sunset Boulevard: America as Brought You by the People Who Make Television* (New York, 1979), p. 98.
27. "Interview with Walter Cronkite: A Candid Conversation with America's Most Trusted Newsman," *Playboy*, June 1973, p. 76, cited by Rothman, op. cit., p. 364.
28. Ibid., p. 386.
29. Michael J. Robinson, "Public Affairs Television and the Growth of Political Malaise: The Case of 'The Selling of the Pentagon,'" *American Political Science Review*, LXX (1976): 425, 427, 429.
30. Martin H. Seiden, *Who Controls the Mass Media? Popular Myths and Economic Realities* (New York, 1974), p. 144; see also Robert J. Glessing, *The Underground Press* (Bloomington, Ind., 1970).
31. Cf. Thomas M. McNulty, "Vietnam Specials: Policy and Content," *Journal of Communication*, XXV (1975): 173–80; Michael J. Arlen, *Living-room War* (New York, 1969), p. 45.
32. David H. Halberstam, "CBS: The Power and the Profits," *Atlantic Monthly* (February 1976), p. 74.
33. Robert Paul Wolff, *The Poverty of Liberalism* (Boston, 1968), p. 113.

34. See on this the massive study of Peter Braestrup, *Big Story: How the American Press and Television Reported and Interpreted the Crisis of Tet 1968 in Vietnam and Washington*, 2 vols. (Boulder, Colo., 1977).
35. Don Oberdorfer, *Tet!* (Garden City, N.Y., 1971), p. 238.
36. Halberstam, op. cit., p. 81.
37. Quoted in Edward Jay Epstein, "The War in Vietnam: What Happened vs. What We Saw," *TV Guide*, reprint of a three-part series in September-October 1973, p. 11.
38. Oberdorfer, op. cit., p. 241.
39. For some striking examples of the credulity of the media, see Guenter Lewy, *America in Vietnam* (New York, 1978), pp. 321–24.
40. See, e.g., Ernest W. Lefever, *TV and National Defense: An Analysis of CBS News, 1972–1973* (Boston, Va., 1974) and the criticisms of this study by Robert S. Frank, "The IAS Case Against CBS," *Journal of Communication*, XXV (1975): 186–89, and Fred W. Friendly, *The Good Guys, the Bad Guys and the First Amendment* (New York, 1976), pp. 174–80.
41. Cf. Hoffstetter, op. cit., pp. 88, 172–73; American Institute for Political Communication, *"Liberal Bias" as a Factor in Network Television News Reporting* (Washington, D.C., 1972); Richard A. Pride and Gary L. Wamsley, "Symbol Analysis of Network Coverage of Laos Incursion," *Journalism Quarterly*, IXL (1972): 640.
42. This study is discussed by Davison, op. cit., p. 165.
43. William P. Gerberding, "The Politics of the Alienated Left: An Assessment," in William P. Gerberding and Duane E. Smith, eds., *The Radical Left: The Abuse of Discontent* (Boston, 1970), p. 324.
44. Quoted in Epstein, op. cit., p. 9.
45. James Reston, "The End of the Tunnel," *New York Times*, April 30, 1975.
46. Gouldner, op. cit., p. 160.
47. Hans Magnus Enzensberger, "Baukasten zu einer Theorie der Medien," *Kursbuch*, no. 20 (March 1970), p. 164.
48. Seiden, op. cit., p. 5.
49. Schiller, op. cit., p. 83.
50. Klapper, op. cit., p. 205; Denis McQuail, *Towards a Sociology of Mass Communications* (London, 1969), p. 35.
51. Cf. Dennis F. Thompson, *The Democratic Citizen: Social Science and Democratic Theory in the 20th Century* (Cambridge, 1970), p. 93.

PART IV

Conclusions

CHAPTER 8

False Consciousness Evaluated

Considering the crucial importance of the concept of class in Marxian theory, it is surprising that Marx and Engels nowhere clearly defined what they meant by this term. At times, they considered a social class constituted by the function of its members in the process of production — by the sharing of economic conditions. Landowners, for example, on occasion are thus regarded as a class. At other times, Marx and Engels stressed the subjective awareness of common interests. The French peasants, Marx observed, lived under similar economic conditions "which separate their mode of life, their interests and their culture from those of other classes, and put them in hostile opposition to the latter," and, in this sense, "they form a class." But inasmuch as "the identity of their interests begets no community, no national bond and no political organization among them, they do not form a class."[1] The peasants, in the terminology of Marx's *Poverty of Philosophy*, were a class marked off from other classes, but they were not yet a class for itself. In other words, according to this second usage, a class becomes a social class in the full meaning of the term only when its members are linked by the tie of class consciousness, by sharing an awareness of their common political interests.[2]

The Problem of Class Interests

This dual conception of class is the basis of the Marxian notion of false consciousness as it applies to the proletariat. Workers were falsely conscious, Marx and Engels believed, if they did not yet understand their true class interests, if they did not grasp that an achievement and realization of these interests required the overthrow of the capitalist system. As we have seen earlier, Marx and Engels expected that the proletariat would eventually acquire revolutionary consciousness and thus fulfill the ideal type of a social class. But this process of "maturation" has not taken place, and in order to explain why this crucial Marxian prophecy has been disappointed it is necessary to do more than invoke the allegedly uprooted alienated existence of man in contemporary society and his indulgence in mass culture that are said to prevent the worker from striving to achieve the great dream

113

of a transfigured humanity. Much of this criticism of modern man and mass culture, as Edward Shils has appropriately noted, is a product of "vague aspirations for an unrealizable ideal, resentment against American society, and, at bottom, romanticism dressed up in the language of sociology, psychoanalysis, and existentialism."[3] In order to account for the failure of the working class to fulfill the revolutionary vocation with which Marxism has endowed it, it is also not enough simply to accuse the workers of having been "bought off from humanitarian concerns [by] the present system of affluence" that has created "false consciousness."[4] This kind of analysis, after all, amounts to little more than the affixing of labels.

Most non-Marxian sociologists distinguish between the objective facts of social stratifiction and social inequality, on one hand, and the subjective phenomenon of class membership on the other. The former can be described with the aid of empirical categories — people have different occupations and manners as well as different amounts of wealth and power. The latter involves an individual's loyalties and values, a subjective kind of membership devoid of external or objective insignia.[5] Two important consequences follow from this view of social reality. First, the objective facts of social stratification are not necessarily linked to the subjective notion of class. A factory worker may or may not consider himself a member of the working class. It is not logically contradictory to speak of the children of workers, or workers themselves, aspiring to middle-class status. Secondly, even members of the same class do not necessarily share a common political outlook, and, in the absence of unanimity, it is presumptuous to speak of the "objective" or "real" interests of a class. Englishmen who think of themselves as members of the working class may see their best interests served by supporting the programs of either the Communist or Labor or Liberal or Conservative party. German workers may consider it in their interest to vote for the Christian Democrats just as American workers may decide to support a Republican candidate for Congress or the presidency. The lowly clerk or secretary or young worker whose ambition it is to become the owner of his own business may have a realistic or unrealistic understanding of his chances for social advancement, but unless he lives in a static society where social mobility is completely foreclosed, he cannot be said to be acting irrationally or contrary to the "real" interests of his class. There are no true ideologies appropriate for a given class; there are no such things as "correct class interests" or "correct class consciousness." What is best for one's class can always be the subject of rational argument.

The great advantage of this non-Marxian analysis of society is that it enables us to make sense of political realities without introducing arbitrary and philosophically dubious categories such as false consciousness or the verdict of history. Under this view it is no longer a puzzle why workers in the advanced capitalist countries lack the revolutionary class consciousness expected of them by Marx and Engels, for we had no reason to assume the emergence of such a class consciousness in the first place. To the non-Marxist, there are no inevitable laws of history that move mankind toward a predetermined goal, and the historical mission of the proletariat is a myth. The Marxian notions that the proletariat alone is privy to moral truth and that its ideological beliefs — or, better, the beliefs its mentors have decreed it *ought* to hold — alone represent the best interests of humanity are similarly unsupported by any kind of evidence. Indeed, why should the position of a class in the social structure validate the political beliefs of that class?

Empirical studies of public opinion and political behavior show that the same social environment does not necessarily create a common political perspective. As a result of the primary socialization, which the individual undergoes in the family, and in consequence of the "biographically rooted idiosyncrasies," which are created in these early years, a "lower-class perspective may induce a mood of contentment, resignation, bitter resentment, or seething rebelliousness."[6] Moreover, in addition to economic interests, individuals are motivated by considerations of religion, race, region, ethnicity or lifestyle. The one-third of British manual workers who consistently vote Conservative may do so because they have greater confidence in the ability of the Conservative party to manage the economy or because they like the artistocratic style of the Tories. The psychological satisfaction derived from voting with the class with which they identify may outweigh the material benefits expected from a vote for the Labor party.[7] Lastly, political consciousness may be shaped by common experiences at the work place. A female secretary may come to admire her boss because of his personality and looks or his ability to run his business, and she may adopt the boss's political views rather than those of the union to which she belongs.

False Consciousness Revised

Most contemporary radicals do not deny the empirical fact that individuals make political choices on grounds other than social class exclusively, and many of them no longer associate that which is desirable with the interests of any one class. Instead, and in line with the "critical theory" of the Frankfurt school, they develop a theory of false consciousness based on the failure of contemporary man to recognize his "real" needs. "By false consciousness or systematic misunderstandings," writes the philosopher Brian Fay, "the critical theorist means a set of interrelated illusions about human needs, about the nature of human happiness, about what is good and of value, and about how one should act in relation with others to achieve these things." Much human misery is socially caused, "a great deal of suffering is the result of people unwittingly cooperating to produce it because they do not know their true needs and are unable to discover them, of structures of authority which have their power only because their unhappy victims are unaware of the ways in which they are participating in their own victimization."[8] According to Jürgen Habermas, both Marx and Freud incorporate an interest in emancipation. Just as the analyst can initiate a process of self-reflection that will lead to the emancipation of the patient from unrecognized dependencies, so the social critic can enlighten oppressed groups about their true interests. He can initiate self-reflection that will seek to overcome "systematic distortions of communication" and which can lead to mature autonomy and responsibility on the part of large groups of people.[9]

The prescriptions of the Frankfurt school for emancipation from false consciousness appear to raise several difficulties. There is first the problem of defining "true" human needs. Apart from certain elementary require-ments essential for sheer survival — food, clothing, shelter, etc. — social scientists are unable to agree on what man's true needs are. Man is a social animal and there is no humanity apart from society. Hence there exist nu-merous ways of being human and fulfilling man's needs. For example, some theorists reject aggressive behavior as a false need, others welcome conflict, struggle, and tension as creative manifestations of the human per-sonality. Moreover, many human needs are not mutually compatible. The resolution of such disagreements may not be possible on the cognitive plane; the existence of certain needs is not determinative of their moral quality. It is neither self-contradictory nor logically odd to oppose the satis-faction of needs (conative dispositions) that we consider morally undesir-able such as a need for success or drugs, for example.[10]

Secondly, the attempt of Jürgen Habermas to draw an analogy between the analyst-patient relationship and that of the social critic and oppressed social groups involves additional problems. As Habermas himself recog-nized, the analysis of a patient will not succeed unless the patient experi-ences suffering and wants to be released from that condition. Typically, the unhappy patient voluntarily puts himself under the care of the analyst. What then is to be done about social groups that do not experience dissatis-faction with their condition? How will the social critic get them to partici-pate in and accept enlightenment? Habermas has stressed that the process of enlightenment must be free of compulsion and he has rejected the claim of the communist party, a self-appointed elite, to enlighten the masses concerning their true situation. But this leaves unanswered the question who is to decide which social groups are to be enlightened and how this process of emancipation is to be accomplished. This and other objections have been pressed by Habermas's critic, Hans Georg Gadamer, who ac-cuses Habermas of creating a new, "hermeneutically false consciousness."[11] Habermas's derivation of truth from critical reflection, which is to lead to the unmasking of ideological world views, Gadamer regards as an illusory presumption.

An Alternative Theory of False Consciousness

And yet there can exist structures of authority in which people are trapped without being aware of their victimization. When the sociocultural world is perceived as necessity and fate, as controlled by gods, nature, or the forces of history, instead of being seen as an open arena shaped by human activity, Peter Berger has argued, we are dealing with alienation, mystification, or a form of false consciousness. Religion, as Marx had pointed out, has often functioned as such an agency of alienation, it "has been a very important form of false consciousness." For example, the institution of kingship at times was transformed by various religions from a political arrangement, chosen by man, into a system of rule based on "supra-empirical necessities." The internalization of the belief that the king was a sacred figure by individuals who saw themselves as subjects of a divine majesty, Berger has suggested, represented false consciousness.[12] In such cases, social roles are reified, they are accepted as man's inevitable destiny; "there emerges a world that is taken for granted and that is lived through as a necessary fate."[13]

Many traditional societies have been based on such reified social roles. The medieval serf who accepted his inferior status as part of a God-given hierarchical order, the slave who believed in his own inferiority and powerlessness and the right of his owner to do with him as he pleased, the Latin American peasant who regards his suffering as the will of God and accepts it with fatalism and docility — all these are instances of social orders where groups have internalized beliefs about their own inevitable dependency and impotence and are therefore not conscious of their exploitation. Yet in what sense are these beliefs false? If all or most members of a society accept and believe in ideas that justify their inferior status, in what sense can we consider these beliefs distorted?

For people who for centuries have lived in grinding poverty, from which they see no escape, John Galbraith has suggested, acceptance and accommodation may well be a rational response and the optimal solution. In such conditions, religion, the opium of the people, may be "a formula for making the best of a usually hopeless situation."[14] An escapist religion may be the only way to prevent utter demoralization. For example, according to the Hindu doctrine of *karma*, the law of action and retribution, membership in a caste was determined by the virtues or sins of a previous existence, and misfortune and distress were considered the result of one's own doing. This religious belief not only justified the manifest social inequalities of the

Aryan community but provided a credible explanation of the mystery of human suffering. To see poverty, oppression, and human misery generally, as a result of bad *karma*, i.e., sinful conduct in an earlier state of existence, is clearly easier on one's self-image than to attribute these to personal failure in this life. "To the ordinary man," writes a historian of India, "such a doctrine might not appear distasteful and the fact that it quickly obtained almost universal acceptance shows that it met in great measure ancient India's spiritual needs."[15]

To call such beliefs "false consciousness" would seem to ignore the extent to which they are rooted in a people's existential needs. "The concept of false consciousness," notes a student of peasant culture, "overlooks the very real possibility that the actor's 'problem' is not simply one of misperception. It overlooks the possibility that he may, in fact, have his own durable standards of equity and exploitation — standards that lead him to judgments about the situation that are quite different from those of an outside observer equipped with a deductive theory . . . the failure of his views to accord with those of theory is not due to his inability to see things clearly, but to his values."[16] These values may incorporate criteria of fairness that are different from ours but are distinctly functional for a given society and indeed may serve the psychological needs of its people far better than our own normative standards. Whether such values are the result of mystification and "false consciousness" can usually be determined through study of a society's folk culture — its proverbs, legends, jokes, and songs. "If we find that bandits are made into folk heroes, that fallen rebels are treated with reverence, that poachers are celebrated, it is good evidence that transgressions of elite codes evoke a vicarious admiration among peasants. If the forms of outward deference and homage toward elites are privately mocked, it is at least evidence that peasants are hardly in the thrall of a naturally ordained social order."[17] The fact that a certain society has no trace of revolt in itself is thus not proof of the existence of mystification and false consciousness. Submissiveness may be a rational response to a situation of weakness and oppression.

The notion of false consciousness would seem to be applicable if the adherence to a certain view of the world entails avoidable ignorance of important matters of fact and/or the acceptance of empirically false assumptions. False consciousness in this usage would coincide with what some philosophers have called irrational choice or conduct.

For the philosopher Richard Brandt, rational action is (among other things) a fully informed action — taking into account facts that make a difference to the choice of action.[18] Quentin Gibson considers an action rational if it is considered suitable for achieving an end and if it is based on rational beliefs — beliefs resulting from a recognition that there is sufficient evidence in their favor.[19] What do these definitions imply? Brandt's requirement that action be based on awareness of relevant facts rather than on ignorance is not too difficult to defend, though it undoubtedly includes a value bias in favor of making choices guided by careful reasoning and information rather than by guesswork or intuition. Gibson's insistence that a rational action be based on beliefs themselves rational disqualifies superstitions such as not walking under ladders or engaging in rain-dancing. There exists no evidence for these beliefs. Irrational action thus is action that is taken without paying attention to relevant, knowable facts and/or action that is based on factually false premises. Applying these same criteria to the realm of ideas and social roles, we call such beliefs instances of false consciousness.

An individual who decides to smoke cigarettes because he does not know about the health hazards of smoking or who mistakenly believes that no such hazards exist may be said to have made a less than rational choice. His choice would be rational if he had had full and correct knowledge of alternative outcomes, if, let us say, he decided that the pleasure derived from smoking was more important to him than the risk of contracting lung cancer. Similarly, one could argue that if women in a certain society are socialized into believing that they are inferior to men in intelligence and that their place therefore is in the home rather than in the professions, they are deprived of a rational choice and are caught in false consciousness. Even if all women in such a society internalized this belief and fully accepted their alleged intellectual inferiority, their thinking would rest on false factual assumptions and their acceptance of a social role therefore would be an instance of false consciousness. On the other hand, no such false consciousness would be involved if a woman in our society today, knowing that women are intellectually the equal of men, decides not to pursue a professional career and instead chooses to be a mother to her children. This woman made a rational choice, based on an evaluation of alternative options.

It is important to note that this use of the concept of false consciousness does not involve the assumption of some kind of "true consciousness" other than that whatever "consciousness" is chosen be based on full information and be compatible with known matters of fact. The women in the traditional society who believed in the inferiority of females suffered from false consciousness not because they failed to embrace the "true" social role of women. No such role exists; it is up to human beings to choose the lifestyle that they value most. It is no more "correct" or "true" to be a professional woman than it is to be a housewife. False consciousness involves beliefs arrived at in ignorance of important matters of fact or value judgments and beliefs incompatible with known facts. "True" consciousness implies no more than rational consciousness in the same sense in which Brandt and Gibson use the concept of rational choice.

We can now return to Peter Berger's use of the concept of mystification and support his contention that the idea of the divine right of kings, for example, represents false consciousness. The authority of kings can be traced to usurpation, conquest, or consent; the notion that kings be regarded as divine involves the reification of a human institution. Those who accept this belief opt for the institution of monarchy for irrational reasons. There may be good arguments for choosing a monarchy as the preferred form of government, but to do so in the belief that monarchs are established over us by the gods is to act irrationally. The belief in the divine right of kings represents false consciousness. Similarly, certain ideological beliefs are to such an extent based on empirically false elements that they can be regarded as examples of false consciousness. To the non-Marxist not all ideological statements are automatically distorted. Ideologies such as liberalism, socialism, fascism, etc., contain both truth and falsehood, factual and moral elements, verified as well as false and unfalsifiable propositions.[20] But some ideological statements are indeed nothing but strings of distorted facts and smears, much of it beyond any rational analysis. The belief of Nazi anti-Semites that "capitalism (or communism) is a plot hatched by world Jewry to dominate the Aryan race" involves empirically false elements and irrational fears, linked together so as to constitute a demagogic political creed. This, too, is false consciousness.[21]

Should we seek to free and emancipate people from such false consciousness? The answer will depend on circumstances such as the social cost of false consciousness and the availability of viable alternatives. During the years following World War II, women in American society were often taught to believe that they could desire no greater destiny than to glory in their femininity. Truly feminine women, so held the conventional wisdom, did not seek careers or advanced academic degrees. The mystique of feminine fulfillment became a cherished and self-perpetuating core of American culture and mores. "The feminine mystique is so powerful," charged Betty Friedan in 1963, "that women grow up no longer knowing that they have the desires and capabilities the mystique forbids."[22] To be sure, this mystique never fully dominated the thinking of American women, but it nevertheless exacted a price in terms of lost intellectual achievement for the nation. Indeed, even today, after more than a decade of consciousness-raising by the women's movement, women continue to have lower self-esteem and lower aspirations than men.[23] As research has shown, social pressures still lead women to fear success if such pressure makes a woman sense a conflict between her feminine role and competitive achievement.[24] To help women free themselves from such self-defeating ways of thinking and acting would seem to be a worthwhile task. Many individual women may benefit from such enlightenment and so will the country as a whole, which will be enriched by the greater contribution of women.

Such consciousness-raising may carry a price tag. Greater equality of opportunity for women has created new conflicts for women who are no longer sure of their social role. For many working-class women the ability to stay at home rather than having to take a job in the factory not so long ago marked a step toward greater liberty not available to their mothers and grandmothers. In earlier times, women often were driven by sheer need to accept any kind of work, no matter how stultifying or poorly paid. This perception may no longer be universally shared today. Certainly to many women in the educated middle class the decision not to enter the job market may appear as a sign of inferiority. Ideally speaking, women, as everyone else, should be able to choose their lifestyle without outside pressure, whether it be that of the career woman or the "total woman" of Marabel Morgan who finds her happiness in catering to her man, in being a warm homemaker, a sizzling lover — a "super-wife."[25] Yet pressures to conform undoubtedly do exist, though, fortunately, they are not all of one kind.

The consciousness-raising and "pedagogy of the oppressed" engaged in by men like Paulo Freire in Latin America would seem to raise more serious problems. Freire takes it for granted that docility is always the result of false consciousness, an assumption that, as we have seen, may or may not be correct. Not to pose this question is to take an elitist position that can lead to Rousseau's prescription of forcing people to be free. Secondly, while Freire warns against the arrogance of revolutionary leaders, who often consider themselves "the proprietor of revolutionary wisdom"[26] and seek to impose their knowledge on the people, he at the same time expresses a naive admiration for revolutionaries like Marx, Lukács, Mao Zedong, Castro, and Guevara, all of whom at one time or another set themselves up as just such all-wise leaders of the masses and who many times ignored the real sentiments of the people they proposed to liberate. Emancipation from false consciousness, if it is to be truly liberating, must be open-ended. It must set people free to make their own rational choices without committing them to a specific political philosophy or program, whether it be the improvement and reform of existing institutions or their radical change through revolution.

Is Pluralist Democracy Undermined by a "Biased Consensus"?

The same tendency to jump to conclusions regarding the existence of manipulation, bias, and false consciousness is exhibited by some critics of pluralist democracy. There, too, false consciousness often serves merely as a label for views that do not coincide with those of their leftist critics. Pluralist democracy, it is argued, rests on a "biased consensus" that favors certain elite groups.[27] The established values and expectations represent an implicit ideology that "promotes the selective perception and articulation of social problems and conflicts,"[28] and there prevails a subtle form of domination where "those who actually dominate are not conscious of it themselves, simply because their position of dominance has never seriously been challenged."[29] Pluralist democracy tends consistently "to develop a mobilization of bias, a set of values, beliefs, rituals, and procedures that can be exploited by beneficiaries of the unequal value-allocation to defend and promote their preferred position."[30] As a result of indoctrination and socialization to conservative values, people adhere to beliefs damaging to their real interests — they suffer from false consciousness.[31]

This is not the place to undertake a comprehensive evaluation of pluralist democracy, but a few issues closely related to our earlier discussion of mystification and reification must be examined. It is a commonplace to observe that all societies socialize their members into accepting certain values that then define the standards of legitimate thought and conduct. In relatively stable societies these values often come to be accepted more or less automatically. "If socialization has been successful to a degree, the individual acts within the socially prescribed channels with a minimum of reflectiveness."[32] Not infrequently, too, the dominant values and institutions come to be seen as the only correct ones, to be regarded as facts of nature. In such cases we are dealing with reification, and because society would collapse into chaos unless certain regularities were taken for granted, one can argue that such reification "comes close to being a functional imperative."[33]

It is equally clear that American society, while pluralistic and characterized by a good deal of social mobility, is not a society of equals. Indeed, no complex society is. Some inequalities are the result of genetic endowment, others are the consequence of social and institutional arrangements — differentials in wages and salaries, the inheritability of private property, etc. Even full equality of opportunity is unattainable because it would require the control of breeding and early upbringing. As a result of these inequalities, individual members of society and the various organized groups within it are not equal in their influence on political decisions. There exist disparities of power, and while different societies have different disparities none of them lacks them completely. The problem of overcoming cultural norms that reflect and reinforce such disparities is a challenge faced by all societies, no matter what their social system and form of government. It is not a problem unique to pluralist democracies.[34]

The political agenda of a society is therefore constrained by a variety of factors, including the society's dominant values and the entire process of socialization. One can call this consensus biased, but nothing much is gained by the use of this label. It is a bias that appears to be unavoidable. Since the members of society hold different values, some will welcome certain elements of this consensus as salutary while others will criticize it.

What is inadmissible is to regard the very existence of such a consensus as a unique failing of pluralist democracy or, even worse, as a sign of false consciousness.

Are the existence of political apathy and the low level of political participation that afflict many contemporary democracies the result of false consciousness? Are they due to the failure of the political process to generate issues that are meaningful to the masses of the people? Are marginal groups prevented from articulating their interests and placing their demands on the political agenda? This is another group of charges levelled against pluralist democracy that does not fare too well under critical examination. Back in 1960, the well-known political scientist E. E. Schattschneider noted that participation in various private associations exhibited a class bias and that many interests remained unorganized. "The flaw in the pluralist heaven is that the heavenly chorus sings with a strong upper-class accent. Probably about 90 percent of the people cannot get into the pressure system."[35] To some extent, Schattschneider's observation remains valid. It is an empirical fact that members of the middle and upper class generally are more active in politics; in the United States the best single predictor of political involvement is the length of formal eduation that, in turn, is linked to socioeconomic status. Persons in lower-class occupations not only have less information and fewer skills important for active political participation, but many of them also have a reduced sense of political efficacy if not a feeling of political impotence and despair, the result of crushed hopes.

And yet during the last 25 years or so many marginal groups have succeeded in placing their demands on the political agenda, and many previously ignored or neglected issues of public policy have been addressed and dealt with. Civil rights for blacks, poverty, product safety, and the protection of the environment are some of these issues that have been brought into public awareness by newly formed or activated political constituencies. The federal government and individual interested citizens have often galvanized people into pushing for social change. Huey Newton and Bobby Seale, the founders of the Black Panther party, were employed in government-supported poverty programs and wrote their party's manifestos while on the government's payroll. Men like Martin Luther King and Ralph Nader have dramatized new political and social issues and they have succeeded in transforming earlier nonissues into successful causes. The existence of political rights such as the suffrage gives disadvantaged groups the opportunity to use their numbers as a political resource, and many of them have used this resource with considerable success. In pluralist democracies like Austria and the Netherlands, as a result of mobilization by political parties, those with lower socioeconomic resources now vote in larger numbers than those with more income and more education.[36] Indeed, several recent studies have called into question the alleged inability of the man in the street to understand and act upon political issues. People in advanced industrialized societies may not be as apolitical as it was once thought. "Ordinary citizens are, in their own way, both as flawed and as competent as the political elite."[37]

This is not to say that we should ignore or leave unalleviated the inequality of political resources that at times gives an unfair advantage to some groups. Pluralist democracy, no more than any other political system, succeeds in achieving full political equality or in organizing all interests. But the fact that some individuals or groups do not actively participate in politics is not always and necessarily the result of disadvantaged status or indoctrination. Nonparticipation at times may be a sign of general satisfaction with the status quo, and, especially in unstable conditions, high levels of political participation may be the result of general dissatisfaction.[38] Similarly, it is not legitimate to equate lack of concern for a certain issue with suppression, manipulation, or false consciousness. Many working people, for example, may trade off air pollution against employment while being fully aware that they are involved in a trade-off.[39]

It is possible for important issues and latent power conflicts to be ignored as a result of prevailing community values at Peter Bachrach and Morton S. Baratz argued in a much discussed article in 1963.[40] But many allegedly suppressed issues on closer examination turn out to be issues that radicals would like people to consider important while those involved show no interest in them. The question to what extent workers look for satisfaction and personal fulfillment in their jobs, for example, is one where empirical evidence casts doubt on radical conventional wisdom. It is not surprising that intellectuals would regard only work that challenges the mind as rewarding work. However, for most men a job well done and appropriately paid carries its own rewards, whether it be selling a product or fixing a broken pipe or assembling cars on an assembly line. Many people, it turns out, enjoy undemanding work that leaves them free to daydream.[41] The question whether we are dealing with a covert grievance or simply lack of interest on the part of people is one that is difficult to research, but to assume that every nonissue or nondecision is due to a "mobilization of bias" is an unwarranted conclusion and itself an indication of political bias.[42]

Can We Know Our "Real Interests"?

Democratic political theory assumes that in the long run citizens are the best judges of their own interests, but this does not mean that citizens cannot be mistaken about what is in their interest. Their choice may be based on erroneous factual beliefs or ignorance of alternatives, it may be an irrational decision of the kind discussed earlier in this chapter. But while we can show in such cases that people have acted in a less than rational manner — a form of false consciousness — we cannot know what their "real interests" are. Just as the scientific method does not confirm truth but disposes of and eliminates falsehood, and just as the conscientious scholar can get closer to truth and objectivity without reaching these exalted states, so the analysis of human beliefs can point up false consciousness but it cannot lead us to man's "true interests."

It might be in the interest of a slave to be freed, even if he was conditioned to accept slavery and therefore does not articulate a demand for freedom; but, then again, it might not be in his interest. In such a case we can regard the slave's conditioned acceptance of slavery as false consciousness, but we cannot know whether, even in the absence of such conditioning, some slaves might not want to remain slaves.[43] In other words, in line with our concept of rationality, we can state negatively what is *not* in a person's interest. We can assume that most men, given the opportunity, would want to make choices and decisions based on knowledge rather than ignorance. In this sense it is correct to argue that "the most informed choice available to one in a particular context constitutes a judgment in serious pursuit of one's real interests."[44] But beyond this formal criterion of rationality and "real interests" we are not entitled to substitute our values for that of another. A person may prefer the short-run pleasure of smoking or eating rich foods to the long-run benefit of better health and a longer life that may occur if he abstains from such pleasures, or his assessment of short versus long-run consequences may lead him to the opposite decision. As long as his choice is based on knowledge of the alternative, either decision represents a rational choice and not false consciousness. Similarly, a worker may or may not prefer higher income to a more creative job without being falsely conscious in either case. Many such trade-offs are unavoidable. The perfect society where people can maximize all values simultaneously exists only in the imagination of utopians.

The exercise of rationality is sometimes hampered and our understanding of reality distorted because of considerations of prospective advantage or interest. This is what Marx and Engels meant when they spoke of a thinker being unaware of the real motive forces of his thought. Classical political economy, they believed, was "ideological" or false consciousness in this sense. But the fact that people's ideas may be *conditioned* by their social station does not mean that they are *determined* by their perceived interests, and it says nothing about the truth or falsity of these ideas. Personal motives and social consequences are not identical. The natural gas industry, for example, may have lobbied for the decontrol of natural gas prices in order to improve its profits, but it may well have been correct in thinking that such decontrol is in the best interests of the country. A capitalist may defend the capitalist system as best suited to promote the general welfare because his interests are bound up with this system, but his special interest has no bearing on the correctness or incorrectness of the position he espouses. The fact that the capitalist seeks to defend his wealth and favors a social system in which private property is protected does not necessarily lead to a distorted view of how that system works or how it affects other members of society. On the other hand, even when thinking is affected by vested interests, the label of false consciousness may not be the most appropriate. Psychological concepts such as selective perception or rationalization are probably more suitable for explaining this phenomenon.

In a free society there is no room for "objectively true" interests, whether they be linked to a class or be defined by self-proclaimed bearers of enlightenment. The advancement of man's interests involves an unending quest which, like the promotion of the general welfare, has no end. There is no finally good society, well-ordered once and for all; the future must remain open. The just and free society cannot be created; we can only work for a juster and freer society. The consciousness of social groups, expressed in their beliefs and actions, may not be devalued as false because it does not agree with what some regard as the good society or man's true needs. Like the common good, the definition of class or group interests must remain the subject of pluralistic competition. The fact that a pluralist democracy does not succeed in creating a perfectly fair competition does not invalidate the merits of this system. The discrepancy between normative theory and actual practice, between what the system should be and what it actually accomplishes, constitutes a challenge rather than a refutation, an incentive to improve the system rather than to reject it.

Finally, no matter how imperfectly a pluralist democracy may work and how ill-informed and irrational its citizens may at times be, no convincing alternative appears to be in sight. The communist system, where rational consciousness is enshrined in the ideology of the communist party, certainly would seem to offer no improvement. Marxism, which at one time presented itself as liberation from mythology, has itself become a victim of mystification. The dogma of the infallibility of the party has become an oppressive orthodoxy that is supposed to be beyond challenge. In such totalitarian societies where official doctrine prescribes a fiction of unity, observes the former Marxist Leszek Kolakowski, "It has become one of the most important tasks of the ruling class to prevent the self-awareness of society and thus to foster false consciousness."[45]

To prevent the intrusion of such practices into the societies of the West is an urgent task. Some Western radicals who are attracted to the concept of false consciousness recognize that their critical reflections rest upon contestable foundations. Others, even if embracing a doctrine of moral truth, have no desire to impose this truth upon the rest of society. However, it is important to note that the potential for repression is present in the very idea of false consciousness. He who has found the truth not infrequently considers it his moral obligation to benefit others who are less fortunate and less enlightened. If nothing else, the concept of false consciousness — as used by Marxists, neo-Marxists, and other radicals — constitutes a challenge to man's moral autonomy and rationality. Created as a remedy for mystification, it has become the ultimate moral presumption — a new mystification.

Notes

1. Karl Marx, *The Eighteenth Brumaire of Louis Bonaparte*, in Karl Marx and Frederick Engels, *Selected Works*, vol. 1 (Moscow, 1951), p. 303.
2. Cf. Stanislaw Ossowski, *Class Structure in the Social Consciousness*, trans. Sheila Patterson (New York, 1963), pp. 72–73.
3. Edward Shils, "Daydreams and Nightmares: Reflections on the Criticism of Mass Culture," in *The Intellectuals and the Powers and Other Essays* (Chicago, 1972), p. 255.
4. Richard Sennett and Jonathan Cobb, *The Hidden Injuries of Class* (New York, 1972), pp. 5, 151.
5. Richard Centers, *The Psychology of Social Class: A Study of Class Consciousness* (New York, 1961), p. 27.
6. Peter L. Berger and Thomas Luckman, *The Social Construction of Reality: A Treatise in the Sociology of Knowledge* (Garden City, N.Y., 1967), p. 131.
7. John H. Goldthorpe et al., *The Affluent Worker: Political Attitudes and Behavior* (Cambridge, 1968), p. 48; Dennis F. Thompson, *The Democratic Citizen: Social Science and Democratic Theory in the 20th Century* (Cambridge, 1970), pp. 129–30.
8. Brian Fay, "How People Change Themselves: The Relationship between Critical Theory and its Audience," in Terence Ball, ed., *Political Theory and Praxis: New Perspectives* (Minneapolis, 1977), pp. 214, 229.
9. Jürgen Habermas, *Theory and Practice*, trans. John Viertel (Boston, 1973), pp. 9, 39.
10. Cf. Paul W. Taylor, " 'Need' Statements," *Analysis* XIX (1959): 106–11. See also Marvin Zetterbaum, "Equality and Human Needs," *American Political Science Review* LXXI (1977): 983–998.
11. Hans Georg Gadamer, "Rhetorik, Hermeneutik und Ideologiekritik," in Karl-Otto Apel et al., *Hermeneutik und Ideologiekritik* (Frankfurt, 1971), p. 82.
12. Peter L. Berger, *The Sacred Canopy: Elements of a Sociological Theory of Religion* (Garden City, N.Y., 1967), pp. 87-94.
13. Peter Berger and Stanley Pullberg, "Reification and the Sociological Critique of Consciousness," *History and Theory* IV (1965): 203.
14. John K. Galbraith, *The Nature of Mass Poverty* (Cambridge, Mass., 1979), p. 64.
15. A. L. Basham, *The Wonder That Was India* (London, 1956), p. 342. See also Guenter Lewy, *Religion and Revolution* (New York, 1974), pp. 548-550.
16. James C. Scott, *The Moral Economy of the Peasant: Rebellion and Subsistence in Southeast Asia* (New Haven, 1976), p. 160.
17. Ibid., p. 239.

18. Richard Brandt, "Rationality, Egoism, and Morality," *Journal of Philosophy* LXIX (1972): 683.
19. Quentin Gibson, *The Logic of Social Enquiry* (London, 1960), p. 156.
20. Cf. Martin Seliger, *Ideology and Politics* (London, 1976), p. 119.
21. Ibid., p. 159. See also Martin Seliger, *The Marxist Conception of Ideology: A Critical Essay* (London, 1977), p. 141; Joseph Gabel, *False Consciousness: An Essay on Reification*, trans. Margaret A. Thompson (Oxford, 1975), p. 13.
22. Betty Friedan, *The Feminine Mystique* (New York, 1963), p. 68.
23. See the study of Lois M. Monteiro reported in the *New York Times*, December 10, 1978.
24. Juanita H. Williams, *Psychology of Women: Behavior in a Biosocial Context* (New York, 1977), p. 186.
25. Marabel Morgan, *The Total Woman* (Old Toppan, N.J., 1973), p. 183.
26. Paulo Freire, *Pedagogy of the Oppressed*, trans. Myra Bergman Ramos (New York, 1970), p. 47.
27. William E. Connolly, "The Challenge to Pluralist Theory," in William E. Connolly, ed., *The Bias of Pluralism* (New York, 1971), p. 15.
28. Matthew A. Crenson, *The Un-Politics of Air Pollution: A Study of Non-Decisionmaking in the Cities* (Baltimore, 1971), p. 23.
29. Peter Bachrach and Morton S. Baratz, "Two Faces of Power," *American Political Science Review* LVI (1962): 952, n. 30.
30. Peter Bachrach and Morton S. Baratz, *Power and Poverty: Theory and Practice* (New York, 1970), p. 105.
31. Michael Parenti, *Power and the Powerless* (New York, 1978), p. 15.
32. Berger and Pullberg, op. cit., p. 203.
33. Ibid., p. 208.
34. Cf. William A. Kelso, *American Democratic Theory: Pluralism and its Critics* (Westport, Conn., 1978), p. 106.
35. E. E. Schattschneider, *The Semisovereign People: A Realist's View of Democracy in America* (New York, 1960), p. 35.
36. Sidney Verba et al., *Participation and Political Equality: A Seven-Nation Comparison* (Cambridge, 1978), p. 122.
37. Vivien Hart, *Distrust and Democracy: Political Distrust in Britain and America* (Cambridge, 1978), p. 208. See also Norman H. Nie and Kristie Andersen, "Mass Belief Systems Revisited; Political Change and Attitude Structure," *Journal of Politics* XXXVI (1974): 540–91; and Eugene Litwak et al., "Ideological Complexity and Middle-American Rationality," *Public Opinion Quarterly* XXXVII (1973): 317–32.
38. Thompson, op. cit., p. 64.
39. Cf. Nelson W. Polsby, *Community Power and Political Theory: A Further Look at Problems of Evidence and Inference*, 2nd rev. ed. (New Haven, 1980), p. 217.
40. Peter Bachrach and Morton S. Baratz, "Decisions and Nondecisions: An Analytical Framework," *American Political Science Review* LVII (1963): 632–42.
41. Cf. Harold Entwistle, *Class, Culture and Education* (London, 1978), p. 163. See also M. Weir, ed., *Job Satisfaction* (London, 1976).
42. See Andrew S. McFarland, *Power and Leadership in Pluralist Systems* (Stanford, Calif., 1969), pp. 75–79; Raymond Wolfinger, "Nondecisions and the Study of Local Politics," *American Political Science Review* LXV (1971): 1063–1080; Frederick W. Frey, "Comment: On Issues and Non-issues in the Study of Power," Ibid., pp. 1081–1101.

43. My position here differs from both William E. Connolly, *The Terms of Political Discourse* (Lexington, Mass., 1974), p. 65, and that of Felix E. Oppenheim, "Self-Interest and Public Interest," *Political Theory*, III (1975): 273.

44. Connolly, *Terms of Political Discourse*, p. 69.

45. Leszek Kolakowski, *Der revolutionäre Geist* (Stuttgart, 1972), p. 89.

Index